THE VERDICT

By
ELIAS ADAM

AN M-Y BOOKS PAPERBACK

© Copyright 2009
ELIAS ADAM
The right of Elias Adam to be identified as the author of
This work has been asserted by him in accordance with the
Copyright, Designs and Patents Act 1988

All Rights Reserved
No reproduction, copy or transmission of this publication
may be made without written permission.
No paragraph of this publication may be reproduced,
copied or transmitted save with the written permission
or in accordance with the provisions of the Copyright
Act 1956 (as amended). Any person who does any
unauthorised act in relation to this publication may be
liable to criminal prosecution and civil claims for damage.
A CIP catalogue record for this title is available from the
British Library

ISBN 13 digit – 9781906986735

Published by
M-Y Books 'ltd
187 Ware Road
Hertford
Herts SG13 7EQ

Design and layout by Caroline@SparkleforYou.co.uk

A book of natural rebellion...

the sypnosis

To summarise my book, it is an in depth study of ourselves. I challenge the notion that we are the superior race, when in fact, we are the cause of every problem in this world, and like I say in my book we hide behind our seemingly civilized exterior and banners we have named laws. I have juxtaposed this idea by using dogs as a comparison, and after extensive research I am able to prove that they are far better than any of us. We all, including dogs have instincts and a savagery about us but in us, it is tenfold.

   I have based this book mainly from my life experiences and have created different scenarios to show this without directly referring to a specific part of my life. The whole book has a fixed scene that I continually return to, a café that I frequent, where I analyse its clients, my human laboratory if you want. From there I meet a dog, Chiotby that I later meet in a dream. This dream plays a large part in my book and because it is a dream, it allows me to put aside all of my inhibitions and talk more freely and really humble myself as I will be at the receiving end in the dogs' kingdom. After reading my book you will hopefully be able to identify clear links with what I write about people, their hypocrisy and certain modern institutions now. Throughout the book, I delve into our inner thoughts, insecurities, I dissect open the man's chest to reveal what is really inside.

Although my book is not without its light moments of humour, unfortunately my book has a very bitter undertone about it, but unfortunately again that is how life has been delivered to me, and like it or not, although we are taught that good will ultimately triumph, evil has the upper hand in the deck now.

I think my book will appeal to readers who would like to be challenged, whether they agree with me entirely or partly, I am sure that it will at least lead them to ask further questions about relations with ourselves and with others, and perhaps they may even agree with me in the fact that we are the inferior race.

It is indeed a book of natural rebellion…

CONTENTS

Preface vii

CHAPTER 1: Taste of Bitterness 1
CHAPTER 2: Fireworks 12
CHAPTER 3: Whipps Cross 16
CHAPTER 4: The Old Habits 23
CHAPTER 5: Illegals 30
CHAPTER 6: Backfire 38
CHAPTER 7: After Taste 43
CHAPTER 8: The Beautiful Dreams 45
CHAPTER 9: The Court of Dogs 88
CHAPTER 10: The Trial 98

The Verdict of 30 April 2007 It Was 12PM 130

PREFACE

The world in which we live in and this great universe which envelopes us with its multitude of creatures, obliges us to ask questions which most of them, if not all of them still remain unanswered. And the few that we do have, instead of being simple answers, we complicate them into big arguments that only great philosophers know how to manipulate them accurately with fervour. We possess this extraordinary power of thought, this big weapon which makes man the most intelligent of animals.

Yes, we have missed the perfection, but nothing will stop us to persevere in the simplicity of thought.

The arrogance, the hypocrisy, the tyranny; all these are bad gifts which only man can perfect. Instead of progress they force us to reverse and live like wild beasts, ferocious and wild in this modern, cosmopolitan world. I believe that human nature has never prospered throughout time; the first man is identical to the man of today. The only variant is this technology which has become his second nature, this gives us the illusion that we are civilised….. All these enigmas which surround our daily life and persecute us without stop, gave me the inspiration to write the Theory of Existence followed by this book titled The Verdict.

> "It doesn't matter who we hurt whether it be a dog that we mistreat or an ant that we tread on, all that matters is that these are all crimes which we facilitate by ignorance.
>
> The right of living is the same for all creatures, and its true comprehension can only be achieved once you truly understand the right of existence."

Theory of Existence

This theory is based on the immeasurably important creation which is the human brain. Every human was simply 'nothing' before the moment of conception. That was the first stage: the soul without the body. Then it is time for the second stage, when the soul joins its designated flesh. Here, the brain becomes limitless in its power of thought.

It is the same process as switching on a light bulb. If the bulb breaks, the current may not be visible but is still alive. It becomes possible to bring that light alive again by replacing the bulb or attaching a new one.

The greatest sensations of life are feeling that greatness goes beyond what we see and what we feel.

The twins, joy and sadness remind us of our temporary stay here.

The difference between human beings and animals is that animals' brains are limited whereas the human brain is not.

So we all remain as equals in the second stage.

I emphasise that a donkey, dog, rat, fly and human being are all one creation. Because of the limited power of thought for the animals, flies for example will never prosper.

So creatures like animals and insects acknowledge that we exist. They all know the basics of where we come from, what we are doing and where we are going.

The only problem we face is that we do not understand their language. If that were not the case, the donkey, dog, rat, fly would say exactly what I am saying here.

The only sense which separates us and makes us the best species is the power of thought, which when you look at it as a scale, varies between minus 10 and 100 for humans.

Alcohol, drugs and all vices cause the madness and the poor health of the brain to deteriorate; they affect the direct power of thought.

We all are the same, animals and human beings.

It is only when we use the power of thought that elevates us out of the kingdom of animals and gives us the greatness of being human beings. Otherwise we regress to −10 and become worse than animals; we become the most inferior of all creatures.

I would prefer to be a rat than to be a certain type of my own species.

A rat is a natural creature that behaves accordingly to its scale: 1 to 10.

Based on that theory, the concept of perishing is not acceptable or imaginable. The role of death comes to transport us from this life to the other.

Yes all animals will perish, simply because of the limited power of the brain. Why? The soul has to emerge and continue its return journey back to where it comes from.

This presents us with the idea that when we die, it is very similar to when we sleep and wake up to see another day.

CHAPTER 1
TASTE OF BITTERNESS

It was Sunday, a famous day of the week, although it is known for the wrong reasons. Everyone hates it apart from the people that spend its lazy hours asleep. It is punctual, precise and obliges everyone in its presence to buckle under it.

It was five o'clock, a common foggy day and I was standing up defying Sunday's gravitational force. I did not let it tear my flesh, not yet. I was not alone though; I had the power of thought, my pen, a few blank sheets of paper and my soul. With them on my side, no way would Sunday tame me.

I took the bus; there was only the driver and I, everybody else in deep sleep. I could even hear their snoring from within their bedrooms. My favourite seat on the bus is at the front on upper deck. From there I can see the cemetery where the graves are well lined in an eerie absolute silence. The people whom we left sleeping were still snoring in their homes. I asked myself to which world do I belong? Do I belong to the people silently asleep in the graves or to those people who sleep without respite in their beds? This was where my confusion lay, between these two worlds. I had to find the difference between the two, apart from the obvious sleep noises, but was still not convinced or persuaded.

I headed to the café I like at the top of Walthamstow High Street. It is called, Aghroum (bread in Berber). Its owner is Moroccan. He seemed like a decent guy and since I frequented that café a lot, I started loving Moroccans and because of that, I prefer to be of Moroccan origin rather than Algerian.

But when I travel through the big seas and burrow deep within, I change my mind and I start denying and rejecting all that man has created. I am not Algerian, I am not Moroccan, I am not English, I am not Chinese, I am what I am, it is me, without forgetting I was nothing before I entered this world.

My history started when I was inside my mother. This was the beginning of my odyssey, with all its interferences, without stops and never-endings.

I am here; I exist and will exist for all eternity. I refuse to accept that one day I will cease to exist. Before my existence I could say nothing. Now I exist and will exist forever, even death will not kill me off completely. I defy all idiots of all times that my existence really does exist and will remain eternal without perishing. And my soul. My dear, loved soul, born before me and since has never left me.

Let us talk; let's talk this Sunday about those idiots who deny what I mean when I say I exist and my soul with me. Those philosophers. Those very intelligent idiots.

I do not sleep because I do not like sleeping. My candle is dying out and is down to its final, low-burning flame.

I am on my own. I have neither wife nor children; everyone has taken their own path. Now I have nothing, there is only my soul and I on a raft in the rough sea.

I prefer to call 'Dimanche' Sunday because it's meaning is the day of light or sun. Those are the false Sundays because it rains on them with gloom instead of its promised warm sunny rays.

The roads were deserted, the shops were closed, and even the cats and dogs did not venture outside. All the people were sleeping, and I looked like the stray dog on edge, waiting with apprehension. Apprehension for what exactly? I was soaking as I leashed my axe, armed ready in combat to fight this false Sunday.

It was 17/03/07 and at that moment precisely at 7am I was suffocating but managing to describe and express how I feel towards this life that I find very bitter. It is another way to analyse and understand this life. You may ask where the derivation of my bitterness comes from. I cannot tell you what happened to cause my world to be so poignant. It is very personal and the best that I can muster is to describe the endurance of my soul.

That day the sun was delayed. It was late in distributing out its warm reassuring rays. Still I waited but none of its comfort came. I became sad and melancholy. I was and still am in need of those great rays, even Sunday cannot survive without the daily rays. The nights are always here when the sun is absent. I am like the moth that is attracted to the light. I follow the light wherever it goes.

When the first rays finally did arrive they penetrated me to my very bones. I felt enlightened. The mellow warmth resided deep within me. A light like no other illuminated everything, its effect so great, I was left trembling from awe.

This light I speak of, we are all need of, it is not the heat but the light we crave and only that light is what souls and spirits feed from. I felt great gratitude when after the long thirst without the radiance; I was cradled and lulled by the beautiful light that compensated entirely for the black darkness of that morning. I took a pen and wrote a poem:

Belmarsh Flowers

It's Belmarsh, a land with a broken sky
Day and night and another night, I cry
Spring will never spring and die
All hearts born and torn, the love and the son
A land, which ends with quick sand
My heart flies up and down sharpening the sound
No sun, no moon there. Only hearts and
souls shining the air
Son of my love and love again will ignite the light.

I followed the path of light that guided me and made me discover all the horizons of life. I know where I come from, I know why I am here and I know where I am going. My entire life experiences have witnessed and confirmed what I am saying and what I feel; an experience of a man, no more, no less. Half a century and seven years and I have not given up on discovering the world. I am still discovering this world and its intricacies. The world is one-eyed, a scary fiend which wolves down its thousands faces, and trailing behind it, all its proofs which are laid in front of me making me perplexed and in a dreamlike trance the whole time.

I arrived at the café, where the people were armed with their own weapons, seated and lying and their hypocrisy shouting from the rooftops, I know…but what? I was its first client that Sunday. The Polish waitress knew exactly what I wanted as I was a regular customer. She brought me the famous strong black coffee, called the Espresso. The Aghroum was clean and well maintained, the décor was authentic and I believed that the owner of such a café was from Nador and presumptuously a Berber.

I was there alone and there was a befitting serene silence reigning at the café that Sunday morning.

There is gloom and emptiness enveloping the whole world. Everything reminds me of the miners' burrows Areas where they live, everything small, dark and dirty. The sun was there though, prompt, drying the drizzle of yesterday night, giving new life to whomever needs it, rats, families, children, and those beautiful birds singing while ignoring the filth and pretence below as long as the sun is scattering its rays.

The café started to receive its first customers. A steady stream were entering and taking their seats and by midday the café was full and almost ready to burst. All the seats were occupied; I noticed the face of the owner beaming and likewise his customers enjoying themselves. The business was thriving well, it was a Sunday, and all the people were satisfied. But not me. I wonder why?

Maybe it was the bitterness that tore me apart and insisted on my leaving the café, as if it could not tolerate even being around happy folk. However I was not going to accept or crumble under its capricious nature. The light transformed the resentment inside of me after being kneaded and kneaded again until it became dough without a colour, without odour and without taste. It gave life to the hostility. It was like conception and giving birth, from nil to light was like zero to infinity.

I defy anyone who says 'I am happy in this life'. This is an impostor; with maybe the greatest of demons or rather it is simply pure idiocy. Hallucination is the world of the dunce. It is in our nature, we all pretend and lie to others, it is a species of allusions that lead and push people to their destinies.

I am here so I challenged that Sunday and its bitterness. I have light inside of me and my pen wants only to write. My soul feels and knows how I feel towards this ungrateful world. I question myself when I see everyone talking and going about their daily lives: Do they too have the light inside? I will know later. I strive to understand what they are saying, but all is in vain.

All of the customers that day were from eastern countries and I did not understand a single word, so I tried to understand the language of faces. This is a language that anyone can acquire, as long as they have resentment like mine. I *do* try to resist the bitterness, which squeezes my heart and makes me shudder from time to time. Bitterness that has been well kneaded with rays of sunshine.

All of a sudden an unlikely customer attracted my attention; a dog came in with its master who was smoking a pipe, his hair messy. The strange man was contemplating his despair of love. He did not mind about the people around him. He looked mad but did not seem to care that people were staring at him. The first thing that struck me was that surely he was too young to be insane. The dog sat obediently at his feet, a strong contrast in behaviour to that of his master.

The volume of the café rose steadily as the people started to talk more and more, all the time the dog remained silent. Undoubtedly the dog was suffering for his master's madness. His sullen face showed at least *that*. Surely it was torture to remain with that man and his non-stop monologue.

I became more interested in the dog and averted my attention to him instead, like we had a lot more in common than with any other man. He looked straight at me with his large blue eyes; it was difficult to distinguish his age. He immediately barked three times consecutively, each separate time ranging in length and tone.

He then averted his gaze of disdain on me. I understood what he was trying to say, "Filthy race! You're all idiots", and I thought to myself, "what a beautiful creature!" I yearned to be in the madman's position so that I could learn more from that dog. A while later I saw the dog tugging his master, insinuating that, "I'm fed up here let's go!" He succeeded and the master left.

Once outside the dog became the master and dragged the man onwards.

I felt a great battle in me and took to the retreating route. I was bitter because this dog was able to leave; he left me in the café without knowing why I was still there.

That dog strangely reminded me of a person I knew called George who had the same blue eyes but was mute as well as blind, the resemblance was uncanny. I would give all the gold in this world to have found out how that dog became the master and transformed his master into a dog. Something we will undoubtedly discover later.

My study attracted my attention to the rear of the café; there was a man who was probably a centenarian, or close to becoming one. Looking like he was want of sleep, he produced a beautifully carved shepherd's flute quite suddenly. He proceeded to play his little musical instrument to deaf ears; nobody paid any attention to his melody. It probably had completely the opposite effect that he had wished. It was disastrous, more suitable for entrancing a cobra into dance and dreams. I suspect it is the after-effect of all the Sundays he has had in his life.

After a short while he took leave of the café, looking frail and thin as a straw. He was following his walking stick, grasping it by its serpent's head. The walking stick guided him without forgetting to make the usual visits they made to the cemetery nearby.

Meanwhile, everyone in the café seemed happy and joyful in his or her weekly celebration of Sunday. They recount to each other their stories of little meaning and manage to elaborate on stories of last night's dinner. They talked about anything because they had nothing to say. But Sunday forces them to speak, silence is not an option.

It was another sad and melancholy Sunday, although there was reason for it to be noted, one hour had been added. With certainty this was to make it more agreeable and practical. But those responsible are greatly mistaken. Sunday will always be Sunday. Only on this particular day we were made to tolerate another hour on top of our usual endurance. It is what Sunday brings, like the river during a flood, the flood swallows its banks and carries dirty slurry further than you can imagine.

Sunday is here with all its floods, whether we lengthen it or shorten it by an hour, it will destroy who dares cross its path. It possesses the force of a generator, the power that sculpts the things of life.

I was sitting by myself with only my soul as a companion, ready to fight that 'special' Sunday. The first victims of that particular Sunday were all obese who seemed like they were going to explode at any instant. All they knew was eating and drinking day and night without respite even on Sundays, and the worst of it was that they would celebrate it with a feast to honour the Holy Sunday.

The owner of the café I learned was called Filali; I arrived at that knowledge from another customer striking conversation with him. I felt relieved because I knew his name, after all he has been my host for so long, but when

I think about it whether he is called Filali or Hassan, the most important thing was that he is a good person.

Returning to our guests, people now eating continually, they were worse than the 'lazy kings' that reigned hundreds of years ago. At least they had the sense to vomit what they ingested so as not get any fatter. Now we are expanding and swelling without signs of stopping. These people do not think nor ponder, it will be better surely if they had their stomachs where their heads are.

CHAPTER 2

FIREWORKS

Oh my God! This world is horrible and scary!

Three short consecutive explosions. They were rather gloomy and hit a dry note instead of the expected, explosive 'bang'. They were all strong nevertheless. The third was so strong, the flimsy windows in the Aghroum rattled. Everybody was scared, you could read the panic in their faces; their eyes bulged and dilated. There was silence and the atmosphere was very tense. However to the great relief of the customers, they discovered that it was only a false alarm.

The culprit was a boy of nine, a boy you can only describe as round; He looked well nourished, well fed and plump. To their bemusement it was not the shots of a war breaking loose as previously thought but the letting out of flatulence. It was obviously the effect of the over-indulgence of sweets the night before. No doubt the boy felt great relief and was immensely happy and at that, started to bob up and down. If that was not shocking enough, his mum broke out in a heartily applause and looking around the café I could see there was mutual approval amongst the others by their various gestures.

My initial reaction was OH MY GOD! I felt like crying out and shouting but I subdued my cries when I looked around and knew that *I* was the one that was going to seem like *I* was 'out of place'.

I looked on, the fat boy's swollen cheeks started to quiver, and he actually began to cry. Well *'finally'* I thought, a bit of humiliation. He sat between his mother's plentiful legs when she asked, "Darling, why are you crying?"

"Mummy… I feel… a gluey paste… on my pants," he said intermittently.

"Let me see, oh darling, don't worry, once we get home, I'll clean it all up. Now hurry up and drink your chocolate and eat your scrumptious cake before you are sick," she said while feeling for the mess.

The boy then pounced on the milkshake and gulped down the cake, like a greedy pig. Even the boy misjudged the power of his third detonation, like the shots that exterminate everything in its deadly path.

The crazy fanfare did not stop there, it took another dimension. The stench that was slow yet sure to come began to decompose into an acrid smell of sulphur, mixed with burnt rubber tyres and a hint of roasted peanuts. This is a chemical formula that could have killed three large elephants instantly. My eyes began to burn, and I decided that it was time to leave this place before it was too late. In a desperate act of survival, I held my breath.

My gaze averted to another portly, prosperous couple. So big in fact they seemed to float as they wobbled on their chairs, they politely asked the boy to shoot again.

> I stood up immediately for a brisk exit, but luckily the mum intervened and ordered him not to. Her reason behind this much needed discipline, was not saving us from the ordeal, nor for manners' sake, but she was scared that he might tear a muscle in his behind next time.

I suggested to myself that maybe bringing the hours forward that day, might have contributed in destabilising that child's volatile balance. I asked myself, if the dog was here, how would he react in our position? And indeed in that boy's position? I found it absurd and was repulsed.

Letting out flatulence is a natural act; it is another way of rotting. His doing it deliberately in front of people, with such encouragement, made me feel nauseous. This obese generation was prospering. I wanted to run away and join another species.

I felt lost; I could not even narrate what continent I was on! I was ill at ease and everything felt surreal. When I think of that boy who weighed the equivalent of thirteen boys his age in Africa, one thing was confirmed, that this world is vile and unfair.

I took my breath, and almost fainting because the smell still had not subsided, I decided to run away as soon as possible and to never come back to the café as long as I was alive.

Once outside, I took a huge gulp of air that gave me a new lease of life. I felt elated, the sort of elation only survivors of a car crash feel. I shrugged my clothes from the odours still clinging to me and resumed my normal stance on life. I felt freshly cleaned from the smells. I was happy that I was far away from the shooting line.

CHAPTER 3

WHIPPS CROSS

I was heading towards the sun, following my footsteps, which were taking me towards the West. I was still walking in the deserted streets and I could see the entire world laid bare in front of me, still thinking about this Sunday. This surprised me in its caprice that grasped me, but it would not claim me yet.

I was walking peacefully in the direction of Whipps Cross Hospital that used to be a lovely forest before man transformed it into a park, for people like me who frequently enjoy the fresh air

I love Epping Forest, it is a natural beauty, which accommodates and artfully encompasses a hospital. I know this very well because my work used to take me there. One side of the forest purifies the spirit whilst the other side, the hospital, cures the body. I walked and basked in the beautiful harmony that links these two sides.

By then I was facing the artificial lake, where there were small boats which reminded me of all the excursions we had with my kids, navigating our boat in the small stretch of water. My children are now adults. They are unrecognisable to me when I remember those days. This is the cycle of life; we are obliged to accept it without complaint.

The number of Sundays that I have harvested in my life has changed many things for me. But I will never complain about all that is natural. It resembles the beautiful sun, rising in the morning and disappearing behind the horizon in the evening.

Beside the lake was a massive oak tree, which can recount its life and history from beginning to end within the boundaries of that forest. It was witnessing its presence in the forest, but the forest owes its existence to that tree.

I continued my walk through the park, discovering sublime beauty all huddled together or sparsely spaced out, and I felt I was in parallel with this wonderful green city.

The Sunday was not there any more. It surrendered and was conquered by the early evening, leaving in sluggish silence. The sunset alters the natural order of things. The sun was there to make its last touches, transforming everything as objects sunk into the orange flare. It was beautiful; the whole scene was soft and sublime like a beautiful dream. I lifted up my head and saw a small-lost cloud in the immensity of the sky, even *that* was painted with orange. It was definitely the most beautiful cloud, thanks to the orange reflection creating beautiful illusions. It was like I was swimming in my orange dream. It was just me and a soul that overpowers me always.

Without realising it was already dark and getting cold. I hastened my step, the darkness and fear-taking place. I was left amazed at the speed of everything disappearing as if by magic. I had to leave the forest, which apparently ceased to exist.

The following day was not the weekend but I felt free. Like how you might feel after a long hard week at the barracks. Like the Indians say, the 'battle axe is buried'. Nevertheless I still managed to wake up that morning with a sense of regret, just as some people wake up with headaches. The reason being, I did not elaborate on the hospital, and I must rectify my mistake.

Whipps Cross hospital is one of the largest situated hospitals in East London and has the largest accident and emergency department in the whole of Great Britain. I have some wonderful souvenirs and memories from the time that I worked there. I saw, worked with and helped people and thus saw them in all their colours. I was very content in that period of my life. Now they are merely vague memories, perhaps one day I may forget them all together.

Hospitals scare people, especially when they are waiting for test results. We expect and imagine the worst. It goes without saying that no one wishes to stay in hospital unless they are ill. You never see people visit the hospital as they do museums or parks. I imagine a world without hospitals and obviously it is too good to be true, a utopia. But no one can prevent me imagining it. Hospitals are synonyms of microbes, bacteria and germs, not to mention MRSA.

This Methicillin-resistant Staphylococcus Aureus is a beast, very difficult and dangerous like its name suggests. It is quite literally a dirty army, always victorious and stationed at hospitals, a strange choice for a post. They are soldiers without uniforms, helmets, berets or Kalashnikovs; all of them carrying poisons, worse than all the canons of the world. They mock man and his antibiotics. They ravage and kill 3000 per year. It is a real war declared between these assailants and man with his primitive science.

I ask why these beasts wage war on us. It is probably jealousy, which pushes them, or they cannot abide our filth and negligence; they kill us to make us comprehend the need to cleanse ourselves and stop playing idiots. Or perhaps they only want to show us their superiority over us, to show us that they are dirtier and can kill more than we can ever hope to comprehend.

It is a dual between what is visible and what is not, a cold war where man is overtaken by fear. Indeed we lose in advance because the enemy is too intelligent and can often kill more.

I make certain that as soon as I step into the hospital reception I am smiling and keep my voice just above a whisper. I also switch my mobile phone off in case the army is watching me. I have reason for this behaviour; I do not wish to anger them in the hope they will not open fire at me.

I have been lucky, not one has fired a shot at me, until now. Patients live in fear of entering a ward with a curable illness, only to come out with a far more dangerous one, if they manage to leave at all.

Whenever I have the chance to go to Whipps Cross, I mainly visit three departments; maternity, the wards for the elderly and the psychiatric unit.

I always begin with maternity; this is where you hear the first cries of life and where this phenomenon is registered to paper. I had three grandchildren delivered in that hospital. David Beckham was born there too. However I was born on a completely different continent, and over half a century ago. Nobody knew of my birth, why?

Yes, I never had the privilege of being born in London, yet I was born in a really beautiful land where I stayed until 1830 when a huge fire swept across it, burning men as well as forests. That fire has never smouldered and in fact in 1962 it burnt with rage twofold. It is like the eternal fires are still incinerating in my heart.

I ran away from that fire a long time ago, not knowing that one day I would stumble into another softer, warmer and cosier one that burns me to my oblivion.

When I walk nobody takes notice of me. When I speak no one listens to what I have to say. When I want to get married no one accepts my proposals. I know why though, it is because I am poor and ugly!

My poverty that clings to me always pursues me.

The next place I visit is a reminder, or more of a warning as I imagine spending my last minutes of life before I give up my place to others.

The third place, I have always been impressed by mentally ill people. Being with them is a guarantee against boredom. I can stay for hours and hours just observing them and contemplating their world. A madman once in his world is no longer mad. The ones outside his bubble are the ones who become mad.

The person who is insane never admits his insanity or rather does not believe it. However a condition for his cure is to persuade him of his insanity. I will recount to you a small experience of the many similar that I have had.

In my line of work I was asked to assist a mentally disturbed man. I was with a team of doctors and nurses. They were trying to diagnose or at least make observations about his behaviour, trying to decipher the reason for his imbalance. The man in question was in the dark about the purpose of the visits from the doctors, he did not realise that they were there to help him

His eyes seemed to be clued up; he turned to the side and gave out a sly laugh. He was still aware enough though to respond energetically, "Listen! I think *you* are the mad ones! And tell them [he turned to me as I was his interpreter] to get the bloody well out!" Right there and then, for a split second I believed him to be right. He said all of it with enough conviction that I well believed the doctors and we were the ones who were insane and he was the healthy one. Who are you going to believe?

They had to apply some force to make him cooperate. He was put in a straight jacket and sent on the twenty-minute journey, where we were subjected to the most colourful of insults. The strange thing was that his insults were not only very insulting obviously, but were said so nicely. Excuse the contradiction, but it sounded more like art, the offending type.

He proceeded to show off by saying, "All the women in the entire world made advances of marriage to me, but I refused them all because they were all ugly. My future wife, who I am still looking for, will be a princess and we will marry in the summer, then all of those women can be her servants."

He continued with the swearing and insults throughout the journey. I will never forget that man whose story says and explains everything. If we restrain from drinking and eating too much, we will inevitably need to build less hospitals. However we are stubborn and do not mind that we are stubborn. If we are not careful of our gluttony, one day the number of our hospitals will rise and equal the number of train stations we have.

I say with conviction that if there is any hope to change the world, then we must change our eating habits.

CHAPTER 4

THE OLD HABITS

Today I reluctantly veered away from my normal habit of avoiding exceptions; it disturbs my routine, which takes a person outside the realms of normality. I fear they become unique, and this is what I cannot accept.

Today; Monday, the day proceeded by Sunday. I was walking down Walthamstow High St. As usual it was teeming with shoppers; men, women, and children. They were all happy and content bustling together, celebrating the day of shopping. I noticed the presence of people from all nationalities and people from all the colours of the spectrum; it looked like the entire globe was shrunken there.

As always I was by myself with only myself as a companion. It was then that I decided to go against my soul's wish. It refused to go with me to the market. The marketplace and my soul equate to two, they simply do not belong; they are incompatible.

Without it I felt really alone, it contradicted me. I felt embarrassed because I possess a wonderful soul that has always understood me and served me generously...

well most of the time. I have heard that Walthamstow Market is the longest in all of Europe. I have been acquainted with it for over twenty years. I am accustomed to the people walking here and there, talking, smiling, shouting, pushing, and parting with their cash amongst the unbearable noise.

I was wondering with my rucksack on my back just like the multitude but was there under different pretences, and very determined. I tried to read faces; gestures for anything that may be given away that would lead me closer to the truth.

Fifteen long minutes later, nothing came to my assistance. Against the odds though, I remained persistent and stood watch like a hungry hunter. I feared lest I gave up and forsook the market of my presence.

I should not have felt like that, after all it was not Sunday. I was scared of abandoning my post. I mused that if I had a dog to assist me, then we would surely have made some headway in decoding these enigmas.

The sun shone marvellously on top of the stalls. It was the first time the sun had been there, but was not helping with its presence. It shone on me only illusions that the world was perfect.

The depth in me makes me feel things as opposites. I admit I need help. I ask my soul with humility. But it refuses to come to my aid, it won't indulge me. Who else am I going to ask? All the gates around me are locked. I know the key is hiding somewhere inside me but I cannot find it. I took out a bottle of water and sipped it in the hope it would refresh my spirit. Pig-headedness was everywhere, everything was running on neutral.

I started on my return journey down the market hoping that some light would be shed to provide me with clarity, but this search was in vain. All of a sudden everything became crystal clear. The revelation was quite startling. It was hunger, which made me blind and deaf. Let us talk about hunger whilst I am still hungry.

Lest I should forget any details.

Hunger is invisible, it is colourless and odourless. It is an invisible spectrum that exists abundantly across Africa and many third world countries. And for anyone who wants to really know about it must go there first.

It starts with the emptiness of the stomach, before it gradually becomes complete emptiness. From there it starts to squeeze, and churn and pull. It sends out alarms all around the body, reminding the person in question that their safety depends on its satisfaction. This is the moment when food is direly needed. If we try to avoid it or cheat the sensation, it will not work; the whole body system is dependent on it. It threatens to shut down completely if the stomach is not given something to digest.

> *When hunger strikes, then we need food, but what food is there to eat?*

I let my imagination run loose and imagined I was in Somalia, foraging for something to eat, but to no avail there is no bread or water. Is there nothing in that part of the world? Five days later, my powers were dwindling and they evaporated leaving me with no power at all. I turned to the grass and started grazing, but found fierce competition awaiting me from herds of equally hungry animals. I turned to my excrement of which there was none. By then I could feel my guts tearing apart. I drank a sip of my own urine, which was cold and saturated with sulphates and urea. Deep nausea blurred my vision and imagination and everything disappeared.

I returned to the stark reality of Walthamstow Market. Phew! It was a dream. Without losing a moment's thought, I entered the nearest restaurant there was, ordered myself a feast and ravenously gobbled it all up. I had already forgotten about Somalia and all the hunger around the world. To be truthful I did not even wish to think about it.

Leaving much heavier than when I entered, I was met by the same busy crowd. I let them push me and take me in their direction. I let myself be led. If they were not eating food then they were pulling it behind them in sledges as stocks of provisions. They were happy, this radiance spread from their faces to their amply sized bodies that gave them an aspect of prosperity.

After having eaten I saw clearly, just as when dirty windscreens are washed and the visibility is transformed.

Although I am not convinced, something keeps telling me that these people are hiding their anguish and deceptions in pretending there are good times and joy.

Let us talk about what is deeply and stealthily hidden like hypocrisy, selfishness and the thousands of defeats. Everyone has his own manner in surrendering. We all know that nobody on the face of Earth is completely happy. I am not talking about the party of people who choose to be drunk or abuse drugs. They seem to embrace death and choose passivity as their way of life. The rest are rigorously fighting through life. This is the disease that gnaws at my heart continuously and creates realistic illusions. I am not happy. I am always sad and miserable.

What is this big word that eats at us all the time? Compromise.

I much prefer to suffer than to compromise. But compromise this life, this world? I have reached a stage in my life where I can swap this existence with nothing. This life has remained great only in the eyes of a minority of people who do everything to compromise. They have no reservations about even selling themselves.

They are not here to honour the human race; their goal is to stay alive at any cost. They are the vermin. We try to clear their droppings, but despite all our efforts to eradicate ourselves from them, they stick like glue. True to the nature of vermin, they multiply all the time, but until when?

Still being led by the excited crowds I began to count the number of restaurants on the High Street. I was very surprised at the outcome: not fifteen, or twenty, but forty-five restaurants. Their sole goal was to fatten men, women, children and their profits. They are like pumping stations; only they pump grease and fat, calories and protein.

The first time that I was really taken by this issue was by an alarming statistic that was published in the local Guardian on 29/03/07. The title read, "No surprise, one in four children is obese. The alarm bell is pulled and now is our conscience alarmed?"

The winter of yesterday has gone and decomposed, no more foggy mornings or the monotony of dead, silent, black emptiness. Spare a thought for those poor trees who suffered, naked with their absent leaves, like sick birds without plumage.

The spring has arrived; life has resumed its presence. Resuscitating everything that was close to dying. Millions of flowers are born with others pushing silently through the dirt striving to flower. Celebrating in unison their victory in overcoming the grim reaper of cold. The hardship that was winter.

The world is in metamorphosis and becoming nicer. Squirrels inform me that they are scared by nature. It is evident in their nervous disposition, yet they do not feel my presence near them, or at least they do not run away from me. I realise now that it is the effect of spring, its softness and freshness, they too were under its spell.

THE VERDICT

The days become lengthier and are stretched longer and wider. The whole environment develops marvellously. Life is buzzing in all directions, all creatures celebrating together in a perfect marriage. Everything that is, except man. He is absent and is not included on the guest list.

He is not shy in showing his opposition and he sets limits with his ignorance by polluting and destroying the environment. In an act of revenge he shows he is the master. However we know that he is the vermin, incapable of stopping his evil conduct.

I apologise for this Sunday, I broke my promise, and I went back to the café Aghroum. I felt I was under attack from my own resolve. I was attracted just like a magnet despite my decision to not set another foot in that café. I entered.

CHAPTER 5

ILLEGALS

As usual I was the first client of the day, a frugal client because I never order breakfast. I always eat breakfast at home thus economising £2. I am not tight fisted, but I hate wasting purely for the fact that we live in a world where poverty is rife. When I imagine all the people who suffer and their hungry children, my heart constricts to imploding level, so it dictates to me to be careful in my spending, consuming only the bare minimum necessary.

It was 10.30 and the café started to receive its first *real* clients, again all from Eastern Europe. A few moments later a group of young men from North Africa entered boisterously. Their olive skin was a big clue.

They took a seat near me; ignorant of the fact that I understood every single word they spoke. They were all young, the eldest no more than thirty. They spoke with animated hand gestures and loud voices. To outsiders it would have seemed like the beginnings of a brawl. It was the customs of the Mediterranean, probably the effect of the sun, which sharpens voices and gestures. A conversation attracted my attention.

"It's been seven months since I've seen my mum. I'm missing her badly and without my papers I can't even visit her. I hope the English government can get me out of this situation," a man called Jalaal said with unfixed eyes.

"Seven months and already you're crying! Come on Jal, I'm coming up to five years without seeing my mum and wife," Karim responded with a touch of sarcasm.

"Listen Kho (bro), once we get our citizenship the good life will open its doors; housing, free health and beautiful income support. Payment without lifting a finger. What's the point in being healthy and suffering so much? Believe me I prefer to be sick and have all the illnesses of this earth than to suffer like we are now," Jalaal said with real earnest.

"Listen Jal, once you're admitted in hospital, what is the use of having a wife and a house? You will lose everything," Karim said apparently seeing more sense.

"I know why you are arguing; you're like the cat who can't reach the grapes, so it labels them sour instead," joked Jalaal, being the youngest and thus having the last say.

I began to laugh at this well-known proverb perfectly placed. They turned to me unaware that I understood every word. They must have thought that I was insane.

The discussion went on and on; problems, nightmares in their lives. I did not resemble them in looks, so went unnoticed, perhaps because of the long period I have lived here, which has morphed me. With time everything has either been transformed or disappeared. They kept talking without hesitation still unaware that their neighbour understood everything; they spoke about problems, where they came from, what they wanted to do in the future. I felt satisfied, their stories were feeding me and teaching me and I realised that I had an instinct that only animals possess in breaking my promise.

"All hearts born and torn, the love and the son"

I can see why I changed my mind in not ever entering another café. I was privileged to be there, listening and sharing their pains and problems, an undercover councillor if you will.

Regardless of their financial and emotional state, the men were well dressed, clothes that must have cost them quite a bit of money. They began to talk about cars mentioning Renault, Peugeot and Citroen. Their world of automobiles was limited only to French cars. When they entered subjects they spoke like experts in their field, although everything was linked to marriage and their failures. When the tone bordered on depression they reconciled themselves by saying, "Better staying single than staying with a wife that will drive us crazy at the end anyway!" They all nodded in agreement.

We are illegal immigrants, despite the fact that we dress well, eat well and live like kings; we are still under the threat of the English authorities. If our cover is blown they will dump us in prison. England for us is the Promised Land. This is a story about legality and illegality, it gnaws at my very core, and I want to know the truth and discover the extent of the maze.

I too have known this phenomenon. I was illegal in my own country. Over there they kill and torture the illegal. I was obliged to leave my country and look for a better and safer place where I could live freely, and believe me I lived there like an animal! So I knew legality in its worst scenario. Those times conjure up emotional volcanoes in me.

Where are they? The fundamental principles in life, the human rights we talk a lot of these days. Anything firm or stable turns to quicksand underneath my feet. Everything is shaking and falling down.

When I am listening to these youngsters I am aware that they do not know the full extent of their suffering, that they are victims of cruel, evil tyranny from human beings.

For me, the world is going backwards, like reverse gear on a gearbox. This has been happening for a long time, yet they still think that they are progressing. All this technology does not impress me, not at all, for as long as we can see these continents in total misery.

A dog in Europe has more value and lives better compared to millions of people across the globe. Despite the fact that I love animals, especially the dog, since my grey deception the dog is a great example to follow.

Those youth or rather those 'illegal's' have a nomadic life. They do not have a proper place or name; they even hide their names from friends, fearful that they will disclose the information to the police.

They live in constant siege, continual fear; they lead a life of anguish and tumult without end or respite. They are left torn between the past and present, all the time tracked like injured animals relentlessly, in case they are caught and consequently, are finished.

It is a life without a future where their past exists no longer. Their world is always blurry; their world is a mirage, which, as soon as they attempt to get close to eat, to touch its fruits, it disappears. They feel like their humanity is not complete: they are half animals and only half human.

They are the indigenous people of the twenty first century, they were born like this. It is this stage, which pushes them always to flee as denizens, seeking a better world.

Like this I can paint a picture of the life of the illegals. I place my spinning head between my two hands and I looked to run away, to be released. In truth I was seeing nothing despite my eyes being wide open.

This is the common attitude we always have, this confusion about ourselves. It is a shocking sensation when we hurdle past the stage of fear. My tears did not help me calm down and soften me.

This long dormant volcano, which wakes up, and explodes in consuming me. It burns and singes even the floating clouds high up in the sky.

Legal or illegal, two messages which have no meaning. I wished these two labels were erased, with all the frontiers, which divide people into categories, illegal and legal. Ignorance is enough. However when we purposefully block out knowledge and conjure up lies; anger, and then killing is imminent. Killing even becomes pleasurable. They decorate these facts with extravagant banners and laws. They simplify and quench their thirst and greed with hypocrisy by saying simply 'it's legal'. These days a man can easily get married with another and even adopt kids, of course all this is 'legal', tomorrow a man can marry a goat or a rat…why not? They will legalize it. It is the woman's turn; she will become extinct, destroyed and consequently destroy with her man, all because the man was the parasite.

Illegal? Legal? This is the sign of idiots and hypocrites who legalise and illegalise as they like and when they like.

I will never like these people; the mere act of talking about them makes me nauseous. It mixes with bitterness, which fuels the volcano inside me. Then eruption, this is the abomination.

All these wars we see, they are the masterminds of this species that is naturally associated with evil.

It is the same as trying to improve the rat's quality of life. They think the solution is to place them in fields of plentiful barley and beautiful poppy flowers. Little do they know that rats will always be rats, they will escape from the field and plunge into sewage and swim in excrement and urine, because they could not adapt to change.

They adore hurting others. Even more so, they enjoy making people suffer; this is the cruelty of a world, which with all its ingratitude I reject.

I find that when I cry, it is only out of habit and when I cry I do not have tears. Injustice is the current currency that everyone trades in. And like in trade, you have the very rich, who dominate the market and the very poor. It is the same world where some are dreaming and others are living out nightmares that hammer down on them day and night.

It is my soul, which is in rebellion against me and rejects in its turn the rock-bottom ugliness.

Man is not the man of before. Not only is he shrinking physically but we see him reducing himself, by stealing, wasting, oppressing, polluting, and egoism and creating all those borders which impose illegality.

Let people be free to choose what they wish. I do only what my soul dictates to me and I know no one will listen to me because I am merely a poor, ugly man. I depict the epitome; mankind, the wreck. My ugliness is the bitterness, which keeps presenting itself as the type of nightmare where you witness you are being tortured by yourself and no one can hear you, or rather will not.

I cry without tears especially as my heart is torn and bleeds. My tears are invisible; they are the tears of the soul. Oh my God, how cruel is this world!

CHAPTER 6

BACKFIRE

I felt it was unfair to leave the café without giving it a proper goodbye. It was 7.30am and as soon as I entered I approached the counter to order breakfast for the first time. Even the waitress could not believe her eyes. She had to double check.

After that, I took my seat as gently as possible and waited patiently for my breakfast to be brought. It was composed of coffee with milk, a croissant and orange juice. I am not accustomed yet to scrambled eggs and beans on toast, grilled tomatoes, mushrooms and hash browns.

I felt a 'soft' sadness, a light breeze blowing on my soul, marking the beginning and end of the beautiful habits. The sad silence was disturbed sometimes by the faint noise coming from the back of the kitchen.

I was sitting politely, waiting for my breakfast like a small child waiting to be rewarded, lulled to sleep by the beautiful silence.

I looked around, taking a little tour by rolling my eyes around the café that was still empty. Filali was obviously not pleased, what was the use of all that décor without the clients?

The time passed, it was 7.45 am and then came the next client of the day. He had an appearance of a monster, ready to devour everything without waiting. He was roughly 25 stone. He resembled a mammoth. He was huge and his equally huge shirt was worn open like an apron. His chest and enormous stomach were out for all to see. He had huge man breasts and a belly comparable to what a woman in her last month of pregnancy possesses. His armpit hair was like the taiga plant, which reeked venomously and no doubt could have sedated a pig 100 metres away. This was a real monster, one with loose and vibrating fat. He had to push his every stride, swaying from left to right like a massive wild old duck.

I could foresee already that his chair was going to suffer to endure his weight as he sat down nearby with his back to me.

Our breakfasts were served almost at the same time. Mine was served first, but was nothing compared to what was laid down in front of him. It was a feast of all things imaginable; eggs (sunny side up), a big separate plate of beans, three thickly cut bacon rashers, another plate of mash, a big bowl of steaming tea with milk, 5 doughnuts and a 2lt bottle of Coke. I sat in awe wondering how he could possibly digest everything. I almost forgot my own meal was getting cold.

I was distracted against my will. Another detonation retrieved me from the depths of my imagination and startled me. Oh my God! Once again he lost control of his flatulence. I even saw his chair crack under the power while the smell spread all over the café like a dirty cloud with loud thunder burning and electrocuting the air. I could not believe my eyes. The detonation was so powerful and noisy: BERR BLOOB BAH BEER BLO BEER-BEERRRRRRRRRR…

The man turned to me and smiled, as if asking for my appreciation at his magnificent display. He knew for certain that he was in danger after consuming all of that food without opening his safety valve first. He continued smiling a type of smile only idiots can ever truly master. They exhibit that smile in their smugness. He had mastered it well.

After his proclamation of content he began to whistle a very upsetting and stupid melody. He must have felt at great ease after having emptied himself of the putrid gases that had hidden in his guts from the night before. He was relieved but at the great expense of others.

Very quickly I grabbed my bag, placed £2 on my table, and made an even quicker retreat having paid for my small breakfast, which I had hardly touched.

This time I felt like vomiting and shouting. I cannot stomach such sights. And in that final unfortunate circumstance I bid my goodbyes to that café.

I left it running, all the while distancing myself as much as possible from the mediocrity, baseness and the lowliness of man. Those people who let out flatulence and smile at the same time are too chaotic. This is the species, which I refuse to belong to.

Once I was far from the café, I started walking and taking deep breaths, doing so with difficulty. Losing some of my stability I suddenly slipped on a banana skin and took a blow from a tree. I was a bit dazed with a small bump on my forehead, a few bruises and a small cut on my lip. This list of ailments is the after effect of the breakfast that I ordered without even tasting it.

It was a moral and physical disaster in all aspects. I looked like I was stranded in the middle of the sea, the sole survivor of a shipwreck that had lost of all of his means and belongings.

I found myself in rough seas without any knowledge on how to swim. I narrowly missed death, which comes from everywhere. I was at the mercy of those big waves, which toss and play me like children playing with deflated footballs.

I allowed myself to be taken by their power. Everything was unsteady; my spirit, my soul and I. Refusing to give up I held on tight with all my might to the moorings.

It was the most crucial moment of my life. I had to stay firm but the waves kept taking me down further into the oceans.

I was still hooked strongly onto life. I was going to triumph despite the natural powers that destroyed the biggest and strongest of ships; the Titanic. At that defining moment of history when she was sinking, all the steel and iron weighed nothing. I was that survivor who lost the earth and sky, and found myself in my bitter mess that takes me deeper and deeper towards other virgin worlds beyond the vacuum. They are empty worlds, the silence created around me.

I went home that night looking like a tired warrior wearing torn war clothes who has never won a battle in all his life, only knowing how to be conquered and is oblivious to compromise. Still bearing my battle scars I walked with emphasis on my right leg, which hurt terribly. I was after all an armless soldier.

"All hearts born and torn, the love and the son"

It is the route, yet I do not know where to go. It is a war where the enemy is invisible, but I feel its presence nevertheless haunting me all the time. Even running away will not help. I gave my back to this world, where my experience confirms to me a thousand times that this life is not as impressive as I previously thought it. I took years to understand the origins of all truths. There were fantasies that transformed dreams into nightmares. This is life.

CHAPTER 7

AFTER TASTE

We aim, we shoot and we miss. This is what we, as human beings, do in our daily lives. We are contented in affirming that this is life after all. I aim like everyone, I shoot like everyone and the gun seems to explode and disintegrate. It burns my fingers and lips. I thank God, it is a wonder my eyes are still intact. I thank Him that my heart and soul are still present to lift me when I fall. console me when I am sad, and to help me when I need them. Without them I would already be lost.

I felt a light fever overcome me, like the white bed sheets, which were enveloping my body. I slept on my bed with great difficulty that night. My eyes wide open, I was unsure whether I was sleeping or still awake.

One whole hour passed, and I was still counting sheep. My sheep were not fluffy white lambs, but wild mountain goats. They were mocking me and jumping from one rock to another. It was not easy to count them. I attempted to swap them for camels, but there were only seven. I counted them quickly, but my efforts to sleep still failed. I remained awake, if not more than before. Turn by turn I changed my sheep with all the animals of the earth but I could not induce slumber.

The worst part of my predicament was when I was counting ants. There were too many to count and I ended up getting mad and aborting the mission. I was convinced then, that that was the first time that I was properly introduced to insomnia and counting the sheep was only aggravating it even further. Insomnia creates an absolute emptiness; a kingdom that nobody can penetrate and no one can conquer to climb its fortress.

I tried to get round it, by using the element of surprise. But it was still there standing firm. You will witness the sun rising, yet still wait for its drawbridge to come down. Everyone complains about insomnia and migraines. It is quite simply the way we think and eat. If we were to go backwards in time to two centuries ago, people did not know anything about stress, insomnia and migraines.

We are invalid without knowing. We are all victims of a disease, which we do not know of, we have to know if this world will turn upside down and we will certainly see the day that the sun will rise in the West and set in the East.

To understand we must know, and to know we must understand. But knowing what exactly? I leave all this to the dear reader to guess which way I am heading, and to which direction I am heading.

CHAPTER 8
THE BEAUTIFUL DREAMS

I have just turned to my right and entered a wonderful dream world. From now on I will not mention my soul for one simple reason. When I sleep, my soul leaves me and goes flying in its own universe, which I know nothing of. At the first signs of slumber, it is released and has complete freedom, a granted independence from the body.

I must confess that I give it a hard time sometimes especially when I am in cafés or markets.

I am free so it is free, and I will do everything that I cannot normally do when it is present. My soul is sane. I am the ewe with scabies. It is me who provokes it and me that makes mistakes. It is always me who cries. It is me who sleeps, it is me who snores, and it is me who denigrates. It is my soul that stays aloft high in the skies on top of me, lightly touching me. It observes me at a distance. Sometimes it compensates me and at times it punishes me. And sometimes we mix then knead together and become me. That is the best moment.

My soul is generous; it performs this act between three to five times per day. And I wait impatiently for these moments of fulfilment; these are the largest of rewards. It is a type of paradise on earth. But when it becomes angry, it becomes bitterness.

All is black and I do not see anything. I feel alone. It is the route, retreat, panic and chaos. I enter a kingdom bigger than all the skies, which does not recognise borders or frontiers. Human beings and animals are all alike. They even speak the same language. But here we understand each other without speaking. This is the land of miracles. It is the transition from hibernation to another world.

I find myself on the upper deck of the bus as usual; I contemplate about how spring spreads, with flowers strewn everywhere leaving nothing neglected. A distant Dog bark breaks my train of thought, however this bark somehow sounds familiar, like I have heard it somewhere before.

I resolve to get off on the next stop to track this sound. I come out and accelerate my steps towards the call striving for a glimpse of the dog. I near the place where the bark is coming from until I stop abruptly, and in front of me is an enormous house, which has a look of having had a long and prosperous life. I finally recognise the distinct bark; it belongs to the dog from the cafe, that master of the madman. With my spying eye I manage to catch a glimpse of the dog. He is behind a wall. I am sure he is sizing me up as to whether I am that idiot he saw in the café or not.

He slowly emerges from his hiding place and heads towards me. He is instantly recognisable with his large, wet blue eyes. From his reaction I know he recognises me too as he salutes me by wagging his tail vigorously. He opens his mouth to bark, but instead, to my amazement he says, "You are that sad, idiot from the café aren't you?"

I approach him and stroke his head; he seems to relax a bit as he plays coyly with his tail. The first question that storms into my head is to ask what has happened to his crazy master.

It is the ingenuity with no equal that even the scientists or scholars of this earth will not be able to decipher, and will not understand, let alone believe. This world that I have suddenly discovered is a unique one with no equal; a world that I have always dreamed of discovering one day.

Walking side by side with the dog, my hand sometimes brushing his right ear. He remains silent, as if he is talking to me through his silence.

As long as we are walking, my respect for him expands to cement a solid friendship.

He is walking with allure like a wise lion, yet inoffensive at the same time. I cannot even make out the sound of his paws, as if he is walking on velvet.

His magnificent fur similar to a polar bear's, is white, a unique colour among the dogs. After half an hour we are still walking in silence, equal, never as a master and dog.

Admittedly I am becoming impatient, questions burn in my mind. I also possess an immense respect for him. This new friendship which was born fragile paralyses me for fear that I should dare say something that might be disagreeable to him or show myself up in trying as it is clear I am not at the same level as his high rank.

After a lot of deliberation, I finally decide not to disturb this lovely silence, which has created our citadel of friendship.

One more hour and we are still walking. I follow him everywhere he goes smiling at him from time to time. He looks back at me without a look of acknowledgement. I find this experience glorious and sublime.

After three hours of walking he stops so I stop too. He pronounces his first words after hours, which are like gold, "I will see you the same time tomorrow."

Having that same fear lest I upset him, I accept by nodding my head in affirmation. He leaves immediately taking a path through the forest and disappears behind the trees.

I feel a release of sadness as he leaves me all alone. An inclination to follow him wherever he goes grows strong inside me but I acquiesce like a small child promised to be rewarded if they are good. I return back to my home while still in my dream, which prolongs and unfolds wonderfully.

Tomorrow is today. I am here at the appointed place before the fixed time. There are three fruit trees facing me and numerous flowers, exceeding in their loveliness

The time has arrived and from nowhere I see the dog heading towards me smiling. It is the first time I have seen a dog smile, it is a promising smile. A light shines on the flowers making them appear brighter. He resembles an Arab horse, proud and elegant.

"Good morning," he says straight to me,
"What is your name?"

"My name is Son of Adam," I reply obediently.
"I am Chiotby, the son of Kelba. As dogs we do not know our fathers because we do not need them. When we are born we see only our mothers looking after us," he explains.
"My father is Adam and my mother is Eve. Without mother or father we are not seen in a good light, you see… we will be labelled all our lives as 'bastards'," I speak in turn.
Chiotby delves back into his majestic silence, and I follow suit. He is beautiful when he speaks and even more beautiful when silent. I love him dearly. I have a high esteem for him and feel a great friendship has been established, we understand each other without talking. It is like two worlds that meet each other and harmonise hand in hand.

We take a new itinerary this time, crossing hills and streams where we see limpid spring water, running in silence.

We walk side by side, trampling on beautiful flowers, as they spring back from our heavy tread.

After five hours of walking, Chiotby stops and I do the same.

"We stop here. We will see each other again tomorrow at the same time," he orders me, although he need not have used this tone with me. I could not be more devout to him even if I tried.

Once again the joyful prospect of seeing him again consoles my sorrow at our parting and my not following him wherever he may go.

I walk away and enter another part of my dream, which is extending and unfolding.

Tomorrow is today. I am near two streams, which appear clearer than the one from the day before, the flowers in the valley are very abundant. Whilst absorbing all of this beauty around me, Chiotby appears at the top of a hill directly in front of me. The hill shines like a mirror, so that I can see all that is behind me. Another valley covered in white flowers. I become suddenly aware that my ugliness has disappeared and I have become increasingly beautiful from my inner depths outwards.

He comes towards me smiling as he salutes me by taking my hand in a warm handshake. I am amazed by this gesture, which until this moment was largely a human gesture. This proves to me that our friendship is cast in stone.

"How are you Son of Adam?" Chiotby inquires.

"Oh! I'm very well, thank you," I respond, suppressing disbelief that I am actually in a conversation with a dog.

"I feel over the moon when I see you and am very fascinated by you. I would like to know more about you," he says to me with sincerity.

"Oh with great pleasure, but my life is a sad one not worth a single penny," I say with earnest, "I was born free and immediately afterwards chained down. Those chains have never been cut off. I have lived a life of sombre incarceration. My prison is this world where I come from, which was where I met you for the first time with that madman."

"I understand everything now," Chiotby said.

"There are others who wish to be dogs just to cross the frontiers, we call them illegal immigrants. Do you know them?" I ask.

"I think I do, do you mean *unequal's?*" he says confused.

"No. The illegal's are half animals, half human." I say with triumph.

"I am very curious to know the animal side, are they dogs?" Chiotby asks once again.

"Yes indeed, I am also an illegal and come from that category in its worst form. I lived like a dog or rather a dog in human form," I continue.

I watch as Chiotby's big blue eyes shine bright and his torso widens creating a majestic light as if he is the king of his kingdom and I am his vizier.

I return to the subject by saying, "I was born just a few years after the second World War and its echo has stayed with me all my life. My world is a big prison. In coming into this world, I believed we would live forever, but I was wrong. I came to learn later on after having witnessed a funeral for the first time. Since then I have been waiting for my turn. I keep surviving and playing the idiot in believing I can escape death. In truth I have been searching for my turn but there is no aid in outsmarting it. Death is very precise and I would say more precise than all the clocks in the world. It knows us one by one and the worst thing is that we do not know it. We say, 'Life is wonderful' but we are lying to ourselves!" I sigh deeply, here Chiotby evidently thinks I have finished my story and asks me questions I can't answer.

I ask him in my turn, "Do you permit me to question you?"

He replies, "Yes. Listen Adam I have a lot of admiration for you, and this is the first time I have allowed myself to socialise properly with a human. You are free to ask what you like. I think I am not wrong when I say we are great friends but when I saw you in that café, you looked extremely sad and melancholy. The rest of the people there were typical human beings, we call them 'idiots' and the 'irresponsibles'. I could not stay one minute longer

THE VERDICT

there. And when I barked I expressed how I felt. Idiocy is that dirty plant, we manage to cut the roots and it has the art to create new roots, which manage to plant themselves, deeper in uncertainty and ignorance. I left with my sick person to never return," Chiotby continues to tell me what happened on the day after he left the café and how he searched for me.

"That day, I sniffed you out. You were on the 275-bus route, as has become your habit. I needed company because my sick person was killed by a car, he was alone that day. I blame the social services; they were in charge of him, it was down to human negligence. He crossed the road and his last hour was up, he was killed instantly. I cried a lot that day. He was very obedient, he did everything I wanted him to, and it was a very big loss to me.

His name was George. He became acutely sick after a dirty love scandal. He loved the woman in question passionately. She in turn insulted him and his love for her. She had another man who stole George's place in her heart. Coincidently he too was called George. Yet when she was in my George's presence she declared her love to him so earnestly and effortlessly; 'I love you George...I can't live without you George!' She was not a liar but she was referring to her other George. Obviously he believed her and loved her too. She was cheating on him in every way possible. The devastation came when one day he discovered the terrible truth. He found them in his bedroom and heard everything they said.

Leaving them to languish in their guilt, he went to the kitchen, took a big knife, jumped on them and expressed his anger the only way he could. It was a frenzied attack. He left the bloody bodies mangled on the bed then went to sit with his dog.

Since then he has been officially mentally sick, he took peace in speaking to himself. I contacted the Guide Dogs for the Blind Institute and they offered me to him as an experimental case. As you already know we already have a long, well-established association with the blind that has proved a great success. I suggested we do the same thing with the mentally ill. I feel great pride in my initiative, which has made history once again.

It was promising as George was content when he was with me and I can honestly say that there appeared to be some progress. At least until those idiots from the Social Services killed him with their ignorance," he expresses with venom.

After a half an hour, we are still walking and conversing just like friends do when all of a sudden a white crow flies above us, all the while saluting Chiotby.

"How are you?" yells the crow as it perches on a nearby branch, "What's this strange species accompanying you?"

"It is a human being, a friend of mine and he has come from very far," Chiotby responds, "he is here exploring our world, do not worry, he is very inoffensive, you can trust him," he reassures the crow.

THE VERDICT

"Can I speak with him?" the crow requests, barely concealing his excitement.

"Of course," responds Chiotby, evidently amused.

"Hello human being. Do not feel that you have to behave formally, you are amongst friends," the crow says flying off. An intense character, I am unsure whether his words are a welcome or a warning.

"Oh don't worry, that was Ghoraab, his heart is as pure as the colours of his feathers. His appearance is a good sign; it means you are not going to have any nightmares. And in the interpretation, your dream will not be disturbed. There are thousands just like Ghoraab flying in the sky," Chiotby takes his time to explain.

"It is very curious, they are white and not black," I mention.

"No, they are naturally white, over time your judgement of colour and measurements has become inaccurate. Adam, have you any other questions?" I feel he is reading my mind.

"Yes, dear friend, Chiotby, I have thousands but I much prefer to listen to you, I adore the way you speak and I beg you to continue."

After begging him to tell me more, he adds politely in his mesmerising tones, " "There is a big difference between dogs and humans. They were both created with clear and determined missions but we know the human species, maybe better than you know yourselves.

You are all arrogant and you contain the pain inside yourselves. You look down upon us as mere animals because we are dogs. You are wrong and I will prove to you that we are the superior species. Take for example the fact that; you call us, 'dogs' and 'mongrels' not because we are dogs but because you want to degrade us. You keep insulting us, 'he is a dog…he leads a dog's life'. This is an assumption and I will prove to you in this journey that the opposite is true. Man is the parasite. But before this, before we continue our research, let us take a break and talk about our friendship," Chiotby says.

"While man is always in search of gold, I am looking for happiness. I could not find it on Earth so I came to you and opened my heart thus denying where I come from." I confess.

"At the beginning you showed me that you are not a bastard in explaining your parentage, and if I understand correctly, we as dogs would be considered bastards. Once again you are victims of false reflections. A 'bastard' in our world, is a dog that kills another. Like the dog that mauls a human child to death. There are exceptions; dogs that suffer from rabies are excused.

Something I am amazed by is that you call your killers, 'heroes'!" Chiotby declares with disgust.

"Oh dear friend, do not utter another word. I understand everything so put down your bows and armour, and have mercy for my heart. It is bleeding, but I bleed to be cured and to know that I have been cleansed from all the bad blood that circles my veins, already old. This provides me with some comfort," I confess.

We cross a valley where the flowers have replaced abundant trees. The sky is white and bright and there is light but no sun; it is as though it does not exist. I realise we are in a completely different universe.

After much silence, Chiotby turns to me and says, "Let me explain the enigma of our first three days; to leave you and then return each time was to test your patience, determination and perseverance. When I saw you in the café for the first time, I read the deception on your face, it was clear to me that you were not European, you are certainly from Africa. Despite the fact that I was busy with George at the time, I wished all the same to see you one more time. And since then I have barked, until I could be sure I was going to see you again.

As dogs, we possess acute presentiments; we even have the power to foretell earthquakes and such calamities. You realise that we do not bark without reason, unlike you men who can talk endlessly without purpose. I am forever amazed at how you waste your time doing nothing. All that I say to you here can be translated through barks in the other world.

It may sound senseless but our barking has true meaning in every syllable. Our words are worth their weight in gold. Barking has its own grammar, its vocabulary a diverse richness, and it is a language we do not learn but acquire at birth, further enhanced through practise with our mothers.

You have hundreds of languages that serve one purpose only, they divide you and they divide for room to reign. As an English dog, I can easily converse with a Chinese canine friend without need for an interpreter. And furthermore I will never know that he is a Chinese dog. Here we do not exist as an English dog and a Chinese dog. We all exist as 'dogs', no more, no less.

If you place an English dog, an American, a French, an Italian, a Spanish, a Portuguese, and then add a canine from China, I challenge the best of your scientists or scholars to distinguish between a Japanese and a French dog. They will never know and will just waste time in trying. For the simple fact that our ancestors did their utmost to make sure we stayed true to our identity, we would not forfeit our beautiful ways for all the gold in the world.

I speculate also that if they were to analyse the excrement of these dogs, they could not derive their nationality. We have no liars, no philosophers and we have no sorcerers. We have only poems and stories to pass to our pups over the generations. We pass our culture down from generation to generation.

A dog from now is no different to a dog from thirty centuries ago. Our world is perfect. We do not comprehend frontiers, which separate dogs, which are then left to kill one another. We truly believe that all dogs are equal;

this proverb is so true to our philosophy, 'all the pups from the bitch are all dogs like her'.

So far our relationship with human beings, particularly the blind has been documented throughout history. The partnership has been successful and has gone from strength to strength. It all began in a hospital in Paris, Les Quinzevingts. And through the invaluable help from one of my ancestors, Chiotby I, a pioneer during that era, this magnificent two-way relationship spread throughout the globe. My first ancestors came from Siberia and emigrated to all the corners of the Earth.

It is extremely difficult to trace the genealogical routes of dogs, namely because of the wars. The one thing I despise in your books is how you inflate man's achievements to colossal heights, when it is us who do everything.

In 1788 Joseph Resigere, a blind man from Vienna was aided by his trustworthy dog, but people say he walked like he had full eyesight. They fail to acknowledge the ingenuity of the dog. That particular dog was an uncle of mine.

As I mentioned before, my family spread throughout Europe, and I am able to recognise a member by their eyes, by the way they eat and by the accent of their barks.

As far as Morris Frank goes in being the first blind man who introduced guide dogs for the blind, he said 'this article which I paid 5 cents for is more value for me than a thousand dollars' and thanks to this article he could know and discover the power of the dog." Chiotby declares his views forcefully.

Intrigued by the rich history of the centuries before, I interrupt him nevertheless, "But dear friend, what have you done to remember all of this?"

"As dogs, we have a big memory capacity but only with all things to do with dogs. Perhaps this is all too much for you to fathom. You must be a dog to truly understand the depth of these things. Anyway, let us change the subject to something that will certainly amaze you," Chiotby says with a twinkle in his eyes.

We are now flying and on the descent, the ground is a giant mirror that reflects all we see providing a wonderful sensation mid-air. The sensation is unique; it is like laughing, only without the laughter.

My body is torn into a thousand fragments. Each one has its own distinctive tune, which by itself sounds shrill but brought together, harmonises into a sound too beautiful for me to describe so I will surely do it injustice.

My heart is in a light, drunken stupor, which has killed me and flown me toward a new horizon full of light. I remain in this state for hours until my friend Chiotby beckons me to get down and follow him.

"Oh dear friend Chiotby, I would much prefer to stay aloft up there, it's so beautiful," I say.

"Friend, it is a dream I have projected into your dream. You have to thank those butterflies that hover around you. It was the effect of touching their wings. Don't be sad, I will do everything to secure your happiness," Chiotby reassures.

"I thank you without end. I have never been so happy, in fact this is the first time in my existence that I have felt happy," I told him in turn. My dear friend kept surprising me by diverting the conversation to new subjects.

"And about dog's rights what do you do? Man is a vagabond. He keeps maltreating us despite the help we offer him," Chiotby said sternly.

"Dear Chiotby, I apologise for interrupting you. Is it your rights you are asking about? Because it seems you have no clue about human rights."

"We know all about human rights through your horrible behaviour," Chiotby said seeming well informed.

"If I am correct, are you drawing a parallel between human rights and dog rights? Give me an example so that I can have a better idea," I demanded.

"OK. The right of housing, we do not want to live in cold, draughty kennels, we need homes with bathrooms and kitchens."

"Dear friend when we see the false crisis of housing, which is spread everywhere and the selfishness of man, you will forever stay in streets and kennels, human beings will never accept it."

"We want to wear clothes, walking around naked forever is out of the question. We only oblige because we do not have the choice. Thank God they did not beat us in Europe...more or less. But in certain countries, my fellow constituents are maltreated daily, so are some cats and donkeys. I saw for myself their maltreatment in North Africa before," declared Chiotby with evident pain.

"Dear friend Chiotby, human rights...dog's rights, these are what create all those wars. It is quite simple, when people ask or demand their rights, instead of listening to them and giving them what is due, they receive bullets and tear gas. We always see new prisons opening their doors instead of new parks opening their gates. All the time we see people fleeing their countries and emigrating to other countries despite their will.

I advise you to stop talking about these fanciful dog rights. I worry that you will enter wars and destroy your beautiful world, which I admire a lot. Human rights or dog rights, I do not make a difference between the two which are a vision of utopia.

Dear Chiotby. I am sick, sick and tired. I am covered in war wounds from a war I never knew, they have severed my limbs. You will find nothing in this filthy, rotten world, only strife. What is the point of man inventing all that he has, only to be reviewed now? Any invention with positive points has ten negative ones trailing behind.

Human rights serve the same function as water in mirages, which raise your thirst and expectation but we all know we are then condemned to dying of thirst.

Your world is marvellous; it is a thousand times more beautiful than ours. I beg you to forfeit your rights if you want to conserve your peace in this world. And I beg you to take me in as one of your own, I promise to honour my presence among you and I will respect your laws which are beautiful and natural," I told him, believing every word.

I started crying, delicate tears that had a fruity taste. I felt like I was flying. It was true, we were really flying, together, my friend by my side.

"Dear friend Adam, wipe away your tears, I did it on purpose just to get you talking. To release you of the weight of sadness you are burdened with, I too do not believe one word of human rights. We know more than you and we witness all those horrors which only man is responsible for.

"Chiotby, I will ask you if love exists in you world. And while you are at it, tell me about its deceptions. Also your women...oh I mean bitches, do they cheat on you?" I challenged him.

"Dear Adam, before we talk about love, we have to ask ourselves one important question. Firstly, does it really exist? And what type of love are we talking of? The love of dogs is much greater than all the seas together and equally, its deceptions go beyond. In transforming continuously to the point that love and lies emerge and become one, you cannot tell one from the other. It was then that our ancestors decided never to love as you do. And then to be killed later on or to become crazy like poor, George. Our love is our deceit and vice versa.

Our only mission on this earth is to procreate, to increase our numbers as one can possibly manage. So you see, we do not have time for love and folly, which protects us from being cheated.

This is how it is, so I meet a bitch, I like her, I approach her. We love each other for the moment, regardless of place or time. The pleasure is only in making the bitch pregnant. It is in our instinct. At the end she is content and so am I. All dogs are conceived this way. This way has been carried on for thousands of years.

Do not make the mistake of thinking dogs do not have hearts, nor do they feel pain or pleasure. Our senses are far more advanced and acute than yours and so are our feelings. We understand what you do and say. A certain type of love is procured sometimes between us and man, but in very rare occasions. He is too arrogant and does not feel our pain. We stand by him through all of his hard times; our patience lies in our hearts. And after all the countless stupid things you do, we still serve you. A dog is a man's best friend. You lie! Say rather 'the dog is a man's best servant'. That is more accurate. The first man who said that must have thought he was presenting his gratitude. But he only managed to demonstrate his hypocrisy. Man is the most hypocritical of all creatures!" Chiotby spat out.

"Dear friend, tell me where I can find true love and I will go to find it. Dear Chiotby let me talk about love and its falsity which you explained so well already. I will attempt to talk about that type of love that I have never been acquainted with. It sounds remarkably similar to the love of dogs, maybe it is only for dogs like you to experience and understand. I would like an answer to my question, which still has not been answered.

Is love passion? Or is it a rhythm to be played? If you say it is about passion, we can equate that hypocrites are void of that love throughout their lives. At least dogs are more sincere with their bitches than a lot of men. There is mutual consent and neither of you pretend to be something you are not and you do not make promises you intend to break. This is the love that tears families apart and discards children to the streets or if they are lucky to orphanages. All this proves that love does not exist. Rather the poor, ordinary simpleton meets with an equally bored partner.

They meet and to lift their boredom and to create an amiable atmosphere, they fall in love, but involuntarily they soon find themselves trapped in a game of boredom. With no other way out, they separate and leave carnage behind them. It probably started by one smile, a wink of the eye, or some handy information about the delayed train. Anything will do to bring about this alliance, where problems begin. They will head for a shipwreck of the body and heart.

It is the sadness of love. Both nurse broken hearts, both shed a few tears. And in escaping their heartache, they find solace in another, not knowing they will repeat their mistake. They find themselves in another trap. Tomorrow we will do it again. We will repeat the vicious cycle, we love each other, and then loathe each other and then all of a sudden we break up. Only the consequences get larger and larger every time this happens.

It is the usual song "Come tonight" You pour your smelly sap in adding "I love you and see you soon!

Others pretend to be happy but they also posses the secrets of happiness. This makes them exceptions to the law of unhappiness. These people are the worst. They are confused between sadness and happiness. They do not know that they are one and are the same thing. They are walking on driftwood. They keep changing, walking on different, flimsier driftwood at every storm. Those poor people, it is surely better to join others like them in their own island.

Let us consider that love is only a fiddle to be played, and then I can safely say that all people are in love. Whether with his wife or living alone will benefit from that wind of love. And my dear Chiotby, if I understood well your type of love, it is not the type of playing on air nor love from passion. Your love has a mission to accomplish. It does not pretend to be something it is not. I reckon your love is the truest and easily the best. I conclude it the most beautiful.

The man, woman, dog, bitch, to simplify this we should call them male and female to reduce confusion. This world belongs to the male and female, all, which exists without exceptions, comes from this union of the sexes.

A bitter fruit or sweet fruit. We all have to enjoy this lovely and generous land. Dear Chiotby I would like you to illuminate all those old illusions like our world," I pleaded him.

"Listen dear friend, this world belongs to animals and like it or not you are animals like the rest of us. The world will only be beautiful if once man discovers his real nature. He is only a relatively small creature who happens to walk on his two hind legs. He must stop showing off or thinking he is the most handsome.

Dear friend Adam I have advice for you to give to your women, or rather females. The woman should never appear with her ageing mother on her first date with the man who wants to marry her. He will be placed on the spot when he is introduced to the concept of his future wife thirty years on, with wrinkles and grey hair. Your love is carried on and is light as air and will not go far." Chiotby said with wisdom.

"Did you want to say that beauty is not eternal and keeps transforming until one day we are reduced to ash? That today the most beautiful of women will one day be the ugliest, just wait and be patient. Is it like the glorious spring which later changes into a harsh winter, a harsh, frosty killer? You mean to say that beauty is only an illusion among so many in life. Then I was wrong all my life. I naively believed in beauty and its magic effects," I tried to make sense of it all.

"Adam, dear friend the long experience of dogs and bitches throughout the centuries demonstrate that beauty never existed in this world," Chiotby told me.

"If I only knew all of this I would have avoided a lot of problems in my life, and I would be the happiest man on this earth. I don't know how to thank you. This is the light, it is penetrating my heart, and cleaning my wounds and making them disappear in one go. I feel like I own a new heart, clean with a dignity of existence," I elated.

"Friend, let us take a break under that white tree, we should rest a moment. After all these emotions you deserve a break and another dream."

I saw myself flying and my friend was still resting under the shade of that magnificent tree. I was flying in the skies, which have no limits or frontiers. I flew freely; I managed to make out whisperings coming from Chiotby.

"Go ahead we will see each other later!"

I found myself flying alone, amongst thousands of perfumes, which made me drunk and dreamy at the same time. And I saw the most beautiful of things beyond imagination. I wondered where those perfumes came from. Delicately scented and finely coloured, furthermore I saw millions of rays. It seemed each ray had its own sun as a source.

A world full of light and wonder. And I stayed days and days living inside that light, tasting that soft drunkenness of this world. I can honestly claim to have reached the peak of happiness. All of a sudden, my friend Chiotby was calling me and awakening me from that dream.

"Dear friend, you should thank that white tree for the unique fragrance. While you were unaware under that tree, you touched its magic leaves, and it was those leaves which took you to the skies," he explained.

"Chiotby, tell me about your relation with cats. We see all the time a war waged among you without respite and also does the same thing apply to dingoes from Australia," I inquired.

"OK, I will tell you the truth. It is simple ...we do not like cats. It is not because they are cats. It is to do with their behaviour that we cannot abide. The cat is a complex animal. It has two personalities, only one of these sides, all people know of.

It tries by its allure to look like a tiger or a leopard and the fact is, that we know it looks like a weedy rabbit. It cheats people by its allure and purring all the time. And what is hidden behind is what is interesting to know. We do recognise one thing about them. They are more agile than us and are cleaner than we are. But in life we do not only need agility and cleanliness. Life is more complicated than that. We must understand that in order to survive.

The cat has limited itself to those two virtues; agility and cleanliness, and it leaves the rest by chance and uses its charm to make up for its shortfalls. Or rather it employs other means that us, dogs find inadmissible. The cats think they are more intelligent than us and think they are closer to man than we are. They also think they are more trustworthy. This is why we hate them! It is only a show-off and a hypocrite. No more, no less.

Our war with cats is well justified, they even talk to mice, and that tells you incredible things about them. One mouse told me, 'I know some cats who have never known hunting for mice,' and worse than that, they are a really good team, they eat together and they live under the same roof in peace.

And that is not the worst of it; the cats steal and hand over their booty to these mice. All the while, man has no idea of this. He still loves cats and on occasions prefers them to us! Can you imagine? These cats and mice, hunt together and they celebrate their marriages together. The cats' generosity to them is endless; they even help them dig holes and mazes to retreat to.

There is a saying, 'when the cat is not here the mice come out to dance'. And take this from me, I have seen them dance together, it does not bother them one bit. Cats are just not true to their identity.

Secondly, cats despise foreigners. They are against the notion of other cats from around the globe settling with them. The English cat will never accept the French one. They are simply xenophobes. The cat is egoistic, sly and satanic. You must be careful around them and don't trust that serene nature of theirs, which it manipulates with extraordinary skill and success," Chiotby taught and warned me at the same time.

"If I understand correctly, cats are your biggest enemy?" I half asked, half insinuated. Out of fear of being reprimanded.

"No....Our biggest enemy is man, it is he who made cats reduce themselves to their state, to turn them against us and us against them, and push in the proverb, 'Divide to reign'. Dear friend, appearances are more often than not, deceiving. Our world would be more beautiful without this species of cats. Our hunt for the downfall of cats has been a long one. This war was taught to us by our ancestors, it is natural.

Take the fox as an example. You might say he looks like us, and that he belongs to our canine family, but it is not true, it history spans to centuries before. One day a bitch called Dindo was attacked by a wild lynx. Dindo fell pregnant and gave birth to the first dingo and another female called Dinga. All common day dingoes originated from Dingo and Dinga. This cross-breeding is of course not natural which is why the dingoes were rejected by us and were exiled and allocated their own territory in Australia. They are not allowed to ever leave.

The dingoes are wild dogs, they are violent, an attribute that was certainly passed on from the lynx lineage. On another day, a similar event, another accident marked a change to canine history. A dingo attacked a cat, the cat fell pregnant and gave birth to the first fox. And that was its birth into the world. Consequently all foxes derive from that cross-breed. Foxes are another animal we do not like.

They are relentlessly behind those poor defenceless hens, they slaughter them without mercy, with a brutality that matches the brutality of man," Chiotby told me.

Since the beginning of our dream, our journey, throughout those lights, those wonders, and his eloquence kept confirming all my doubts and my problems. With his intelligence of dogs and his braveness, education of all that history kept amazing me at every twist and turn of facts that are unbeknownst to us.

I said to myself where are they? Those beautiful flowers and forests that winter exterminated and torn a thousand and one times and stripped them naked daily.

We all know that by heart, this world that keeps repeating and repeating itself without ceasing. We witness the same scenario always. The sunrises, the woman gives birth, and spring blooms. One knows that by heart, and we all observe, and what of it? This entire universe keeps repeating itself and talking to itself. Everything looks alike, man, woman, dog, bitch, rat, ant and the birds gliding in the skies and take rests in their nests. Nothing is new, we are all here speaking the same language, using the same gestures, eating the same bread and drinking the same water. Who can say anything better? I know for sure nobody can say any more or any better.

Everyone is bored in this world except for imbeciles and idiots. They always wrong themselves and lie to themselves like those animals born late with illnesses that have no remedies. Aaah, how much I regret my past, which was full of lies. I ask myself what was truth and what was lies. A lie is a poison without colour; it is odourless but still tastes nice. We all live with this poison, either ingesting it or spreading it, like the venomous snake which spits it's venom when it wants and exactly where it wants. Man is that rattlesnake with two heads and with a thousand of faces he uses to stare at its prey. That man, that rattlesnake comes and tells us fables to make us believe that the world is beautiful and eternal.

I started to lack braveness of the fact that I wanted to convey the truth for the first time, it was the lie which wanted to overtake me and squash me to the floor like you can squash a defenceless fly with your fingers. I strangle my heart with my two hands in order to make it speak the truth, it eclipses and hides, I pursue it but in vain efforts, I am puffing, my eyes are red and I stammer, oh I think I have a strong grip on it, this time it will not escape, I corner it to the wall.

I conquer the lie in tearing its net and web. It has been growing over millions of years by us lying to ourselves. This world of liars and the creators of illusions, they swear they possess all the knowledge, all the secrets of all truths. They are juggling with fire and the lives of others. They write and they show-off a modesty which does not exist in the first place. They possess the skill and art of all magicians together; I call them the magicians of literature.

Look at that wind which blows at itself and mocks the wind gauge. Why all this heavy sleeping? Heavy in weight, on both the spirit and heart. All people are sleeping heavily.

I release myself in creating a world revolving around truth; I accept that it might not exist. But I still grip it with my hands and feet and bite onto it with my teeth to not let it go.

All the time we see the same old boat with holes in its hull, full of cracks coming to save people who have shipwrecked themselves, without doubt that they will drown them and themselves in turn.

The truth is as clear as daylight, although it is that light that even the naked eye cannot look straight at, and whose rays radiate heat that caresses the blind to remind them of its existence. Nobody can deny that the sun illuminates the whole universe and as soon as we give our backs to the sun, the darkness takes place and night takes reign.

Once again the philosophers attempt at transforming night into day. And they tell us all those stories lacking in depth, full of imaginations with all the possible illusions. From there on, night becomes day and day becomes night.

The poor liars are compelled only to lie instead of telling us the real truth. Truth, certainly does not reside in their camp. Or rather the audience to accept the truth is still a minority.

We can all tell lies easily, their immediate outcome is agreeable, it is like drinking wine and becoming drunk instead of remaining sober and in tune with what we are saying. I will travel further in my search for the ultimate truth.

I come from nowhere, but I do recall my first seconds of existence in my mothers womb; that marvellous world.

This is the start and secret of all creatures without exception, even the great sun and its light. There was a time when it had not existed yet.

I am not mad, neither am I a philosopher nor an idiot. I am simply me, who exists and will exist forever. I will not submit to the idea that someday I will perish, where my grave is the start of that illusion.

Hey you over there! Who is against what I am saying, which I perceive as the truth. It is easy to say, 'the end is limited at the grave and that means perishing'. And that nobody returns from that dark chasm. This is the common argument.

Yes, it very easy to think that, after all this argument is as old as the earth itself. But I must prove the contrary, but prove what exactly? To prove that the sun exists and is not hidden. Or perhaps we have to displace the skies and replace them with a vacuum. It is ridiculous. The sun does not need anybody, neither me nor you to prove its presence. All we have to do is go to the East and wait for that marvellous orange fiery ball, rising in hunting down the night.

Oh! How I suffer, when I think of those youngsters who commit suicide, I can say for certain that if they had access to the truth, they will still be roaming with us in this life.

Who ordered them to commit that terrible crime to themselves? Who was it that told them that this life was so important and beautiful? They take their lives once they become deceived. Do they not know that life may last a few seconds, a few minutes, a few hours, a few weeks or years? And we take our leave and will never come back. I am sure that these unfortunate youths were told by someone that this world was important, important enough to die for, to conclude to him and others that the world is great.

This world is not worth one penny, let alone being worth killing myself for it. One day I asked the ant if they commit suicide if their lives prove hard for them. They did not respond and began to cry, I did too in remembrance of the youngsters who chose to end their lives, only because they were ignorant of the truth.

I repeat once again that this world is not worth one penny. And it looks like a dream or nightmare. Once we wake up we will be aware that we were sleeping. I would like very much for learned philosophers to explain to the young, the pillars of society that this is a world of dogs; we must accept this and not worry ourselves too much.

THE VERDICT

The best philosopher is one who could survive all the daily difficulties whilst still keeping his originality, and looking like all the animals around him at the same time.

After the great purification, removal of the avalanche of rocks and the upturn of soil, and at the end of this earthquake when it finally calms down, it retreats into its deepness and sweeping its burning lava and detestation.

I find myself in the empty and burnt land. A land that is unknown to man, a land without sky or sun. With fear raised, my instinct told me to run from this scorched, barren land.

All of a sudden everything is erased and I find myself again in this marvellous world in company of Chiotby who was waiting to see me again. He was really happy to see me. He started to run towards me at light-speed and hung his strong arms by my neck and kissed me strongly. He was eager to tell me a mountain of things. His perfume was amazing, it was making me drunk, and he smelt more beautiful than a field of lavender.

We cried out of joy in finding each other once more. He feared he lost me forever. All those emotions and tears kept proving that our friendship was still strong and anchored to our hearts. Chiotby could not have lived without me and I felt the same if not more. We sat down in an open courtyard, where the perfume was wafting from the wall of huge flowers fencing the beautiful courtyard.

Chiotby was wearing a fitted blue satin tunic, very fine, which let you see his gleaming white coat of fur underneath. He resembled a fine young Asian prince of the olden times.

A light breeze was blowing on our faces and making the flowers sway which released more of that sacred scent of theirs.

Chiotby began the dialogue, "Dear friend, it is a great pleasure to see you again, I am very touched that you are in front of me. I feared a lot that you were dead like George, I kept crying from contemplating your absence, I asked around all the dogs if they knew of your whereabouts, but all in vain. And I thought the worst and thought you died. I cannot express the great joy at seeing you

Once more, to have you in front of me and to dream together. I am a bit worried this time, if this dream will be disturbed once again and it will be the last dream we have together."

Panicked I said, "Why, is this our last dream? If I am correct, is it you who is going to die and I am not going to see you again? It is horrible to think of not seeing you again in my dream and you are my only friend in the dream. You are a true friend and a master, my dear friend, Chiotby. Once again, I have learned a lot from you."

He began to weep, his tears ran to the ground, watering the magnificent flowers, colouring them marvellously. They were clear, solemn tears from a noble and sincere dog. They were tears that give back life to the poor people; they give back sight to the blind. He stopped crying, stood up and made a sign to follow him, and we left that courtyard.

We walked long hours, which seemed very short because the panorama of the scenery kept changing beautifully, so I was not dulled by seeing the same landscape. I was discovering new colours and lights.

From a distance we could make out a towering mountain, which looked like a succession of high walls of white marble. I hesitated to ask about the mystery of the mountain. We were walking, all the while approaching the impressive white wall, which was truly beautiful, its summit lost high within the clouds. It reflected everything.

We came to walk on a large lake; it was like walking on a carpet of velvet. I could see white fish that were naturally camouflaged to the white depth of the lake floor. My eyes were fixed to this phenomenon, I realised we were flying above those high clouds with a sensation of elated happiness.

The closer we came to the mountain, the more my friend's face grimaced. I read worry on his countenance, so naturally I too worried for him. We continued in a certain suspense, like we were heading to unknown danger.

I saw all of a sudden a flock of Ghoraab flying over us. There were thousands of them this time. Flying in an empty sky of glass. Chiotby came to me and whispered, "Dear Adam, it is too late, you cannot go back, we must advance, do not be scared."

I did not utter a word; I was a little startled at this sudden change. Everything was beautiful then suddenly came this sense of foreboding. I followed Chiotby down a valley, which narrowed more and more, where we became engulfed in complete silence. Made eerie by all the Ghoraab staring at us with their sharp discerning eyes. It was not peaceful silence that we so strive for; it was an empty silence, which made me scared. The only sound came from the flapping of their wings as they flapped in unison.

I had the impression that we were being escorted towards somewhere in this strange place. Chiotby read my fears and made a sign to hurry on and not turn around. We marched on until we reached an opening to a wide valley floor, which was at the foot of that fascinating White Mountain. The valley was surrounded by a massive wall of gold, which shone sending a thousand sparks like fireworks which filled the void around us.

Perched on top of the walls of gold, were thousands of white dogs, each armed with a gold spear, poised as if ready for attack. We stopped here and my dear friend turned to me and said, "Dear friend, Adam, I think this is the end of our journey, we came and untowardly penetrated the kingdom of dogs. I was not able to predict anything. We must wait for orders from now."

A group of dogs all wearing uniforms with blue berets ordered us to follow them, escorting us to the centre of the valley.

Once we arrived at the grand location, the dogs returned to their posts. Racing over the horizon, a substantial cloud appeared, carrying a large number of black dogs all wearing blue satin and black velvet. The cloud stopped near us, all of the dogs bowed to Chiotby, which he retuned in an unusual yet beautiful bark, which surely meant many things to the recipients.

> The dogs all chanted in one voice,
> "Welcome to our Prince Chiotby!"

I was shocked, it was a big surprise. My friend was a prince all this time and I was none the wiser! Although when I look back, it explained a lot about his elegance and airs. How beautiful was the modesty of dogs!

A dog amongst that pack, their leader presumably, descended first and addressed himself to Chiotby. I only guessed his rank by the numerous medals on his chest. He began with a slow, low bow, a respectful bow whose duration was evidence of the esteem he held for Chiotby. They began to talk or whisper, irrelevant to me, as I understood nothing anyway. I was drawn to this great meeting; I found the scene very emotional.

Again the dogs started to bark. The barking looked very much in soft symphony; I fancied it was their national anthem. I was again very fascinated by this marvellous universe of the dogs. To my surprise although by now I should have been more accustomed to them,

I turned to see Chiotby in a change of clothes. My jaws were wide open; he looked distinguished over the others and looked like a real prince. He wore a long trailing robe, embroidered in red and green and was sat on a massive throne of solid, sculptured gold. It looked like a big tree sending out fluorescent light like a soft glowing fire. On top of his head was a crown of green gold circled by a green fire, which illuminated the crown even more. I had never seen anything so amazing in all my life.

After a long discussion between Chiotby and the leaders, Chiotby made a sign for them not to follow him and came to me. It was another Chiotby, I could not recognise him, he was sublime and beautiful, his walk changed, his look more splendid, his gaze deeper, his voice softer, more musical, every time he spoke I compared his voice to a thousand of violins.

My love for him and respect increased more and more.

"Dear friend, Adam, I apologise for all the opulence you see on me. I do not have a choice. As you see now, I am a prince and I must follow the protocol of my ancestors and princes before me. This dog you see is, Nazero, he is a general, he alone commands three million dogs and he is here to welcome me after my lengthy stay away and return to my kingdom."

Chiotby explained that he must leave me for a period of time, and that he had no choice, I remained by myself or rather surrounded by a pack of fifty dogs wearing white and green uniforms, they looked very much like guards of honour.

When I looked at them, and smiled, they lowered their gaze. I stayed hours and hours contemplating this world of dogs. I felt pleasure, soft and comforting and re-comforting.

I allowed myself to be taken by that soft, agreeable breeze, all the time making me feel intoxicated by its unique perfume, I instantly beheld myself flying by the flank of the guard dogs of honour. They manoeuvred behind me with smiling, downcast eyes. I could barely make out a big cloud peeping through the horizon but even at a disadvantaged distance I could distinguish the form of my friend the Prince seated on his throne, with thousands of more white dogs, marvellously dressed surrounding him. Above that cloud, was a fierce fire, red with a green centre illuminating the entire surface of the cloud and spotlighting the throne.

Chiotby came down the cloud and ran towards me with wide arms and an assault of kisses. The dogs all lowered their gazes and did not flinch a muscle, like they were white marble statues. He bid me sit next to him on his throne. The cloud took off again and started for that mysterious white wall. Every time we seemed to make progress it still seamed far away, just to illustrate its magnitude.

I felt like the whole world moved and travelled above clouds. The sensation was great; it was like we were flying on a fluffy, magic carpet. We reached our destinations in what seemed to be like seconds on top of the great long wall that stretched to your right and left as far as the eye could see. A cloud of yellow dust seemed to meet us immediately. Which enveloped us, Chiotby later explained that it was the air that they breathe in his kingdom. That air was so sweet that I feared I was going to hyperventilate because I wanted to take in deeper breaths more often. The more I breathed, the more I felt intoxicated, and I found myself in yet another dream, more beautiful than the previous one, until my friend the Prince touched me and woke me up from that great sensation and announced that we had reached our final destination.

I felt like my heart was going to explode out of joy and happiness. We came down onto a city where the flowers let out a multitude of lights and another light came from the sky immersing everything in its hue. A soft, but thick fog, which was very fine and transparent. The ground was clear blue and soft like a carpet of velvet. When we walked, we let out behind us perfumed steam. My friend the Prince turned to me and told me, "Dear friend, I must leave you once again, have a rest until I come back for you."

I did not need to be told twice, his speech was so nice, disagreeing was futile, I longed to live my life there than live in the man's filthy, rotten world.

I took advantage of the Prince's absence by exploring the magic kingdom, which was still fascinating me. I saw roses big as trees, I saw palm trees with flowers instead of dates, I saw fish swimming in rivers without water. I saw snakes emptying their venom. I saw lions, gazelles, hyenas, foxes, hens, all living together, talking together in beautiful harmony. I was amazed at these spectacles. They all returned my confused face with smiles as if they were acquainted with them. What I was seeing was unbelievable. I needed hours and hours to contemplate the wonders of this kingdom. I almost forgot my friend the Prince coming towards with his guards of honour behind him.

"Dear friend how do you find my kingdom?" he asked me failing to hide his pride.

"I cannot find the words to express what I am seeing in front of me. But one thing I can say is that it is a thousand times better than the world of man," I managed to articulate with great difficulty.

"Dear friend, tonight you are going to spend the night at my house and tomorrow morning, I have a big surprise which could be either very good or bad," he said and took off, leaving me excited and perturbed.

I asked myself whether it was possible to see any negatives in this kingdom. As far as my experiences here go, they have gotten better and better.

The next time we met, we were alone. We were travelling on the cloud again and the guards remained, they were discharged and were at ease. He invited me to sit with him on his throne that was one solid, sculptured piece of diamond, with flowers embedded into it. Their roots were inside at the bottom of the diamond throne. It seemed like we were part of the jewel.

We flew very high until we arrived near another big cloud that had a platform of green velvet. We landed on the platform which was a great carpet covering an immense area of thousands of hectares.

"Dear friend, what you are seeing here is my palace, I inherited it from my ancestors. This palace looked empty. We could not see anyone, not one single dog around. All of a sudden I felt the soil from underneath me open and it swallowed us inside. The surprise is what lay in store, we found ourselves in an orchard with its fruit trees upside-down, and they were suspended in thin air, with their roots pointing upwards and their branches heavy with fruit at the bottom. I needed only to extend my hand to pick and choose at the huge array of fruit available. I began to fidget.

There were rivers weaving in and out of the trees everywhere. We trod in that water, however we were not wet. This place was enchanting.

Later, my friend the Prince suggested we eat something, I forgot my own hunger, but as he mentioned it then, I was scared I could never satisfy it with all the beautiful fruit displayed. We sat under the shade of a large grape vine, whose leaves spread in the sky. Each grape was the size of a watermelon. Any fruit that I fancied found its own way to my lap. It was a true feast; grapes, figs of all colours, oranges, melons of all sorts and many I could not name. I began with the grape; each was like a pouch of grape juice. It was delicious and perfumed. I pounced on the fruit like a starved person. It was the first time in all my life that I saw such quantity of fruit.

My hunger fully satisfied I slept that night under the tree and entered another dream which was again more beautiful than the previous. It was the best of all the dreams I had. I must omit its details because I could not find the words to describe the feelings I felt in it. It was a dream beyond the normal dreams we have, it surpassed man's imagination and I believe that our brain is limited in creating such a marvel in sleep. It was something I was not aware that our human brain was able to conjure up.

The next day, I rose and found Chiotby patient by my side. We prepared ourselves for another departure of the palace although I was more content to spend my whole life in it. We headed towards the horizon. The guards of honour approached us fast and took their places behind us. We arrived at an enormous structure, it had an equally huge gate and on top of the gates was a bust of a dog, its torso was of a dog with a lion's mane and it had wings of a vulture spanning far. I wished to know the significance of the emblem, dog, lion and vulture until the Prince guessed my thoughts and said to me, "Dear friend, this is the emblem which represents our justice system and tribunals."

CHAPTER 9

THE COURT OF DOGS

Quite suddenly, it all dawned on me, I understood. I felt something strange and dodgy going on. And this thing was directed at me, like a plot against me. But I tried to put that gnawing doubt out of my head, I still had my great friendship with the Prince to hold onto, I needn't worry. He would not let me down.

I was desperate for an explanation; I sensed Chiotby's awkwardness when he opened his mouth to say, "Dear friend, I have to announce some bad news to you despite my will. Before I tell you, do not forget that we will always remain good friends and that you can always rely on me...My dears friends the Great Council of the Wise have decided to prosecute you and judge you over all the crimes committed by the humans on Earth. It cannot be helped even though you are my best friend and I know you are the most pacifying person on the face of the Earth. However the rest of the dogs cannot be sure of that because nobody knows you. I am afraid it is up to the tribunal. The Crown Court which is going to take your case up will see if you are guilty or innocent despite I may stress, I believe you are innocent."

I felt a flurry of emotions, bewilderment, anger, and fatigue. Once again I took my head between my hands, the relentless life has inevitably tracked me down and caught up with me...even here. This was not the first time I was blindly called to court as the defendant. I was already tagged with three charges, two of those were death penalties and one was a life sentence. The judges were men who sentenced me to death without even setting their eyes on me or knowing me. But who tries the judges and the kings? Certainly nobody or by another law overtaking all laws... Who will prove my innocence, the innocence of the innocence certainly no one again. I plead guilty, I deserve to be hanged or thrown into the dungeons for a thousand years or more.

Man is that sick child as long as the ignorance is still there; the oppression of others will never be extinguished. Only a philosopher could reach the adult age, but only after problems and a dose of madness. I will go as far as to say that all the mad people in the world are philosophers and they want to say to tell us important things, which we cannot and will not understand. We then lock them up and admit they are right.

I was young once. I wanted to clean the streets out of benevolence. So I took a broom and started to clean away the filth, until one day I was ordered to stop cleaning. The men responded to me rudely, 'We are the sweepers and only we can sweep the roads.' But I contested, 'Let me help you at least, there is too much rubbish for you to clean all by yourselves.' All of sudden they chained me and threw me into prison. It was only until later that I understood everything. Those false sweepers were nocturnal, they came out at night whilst everyone was asleep, they then dumped the rubbish on the ground, so that in the morning all the people see is that they are clearing away the rubbish. They seemed to be hard-working, productive, helpful people, and the people were grateful. Those false sweepers not only were lying but they were paid two salaries, one for the night shift and another for the day. It was them who condemned me to two consecutive deaths.

The two verdicts of the trial were; I was a parasite and I was the one making the city streets dirty. Thank God that I escaped safely!

As I am but a poor man, I did not have any lawyers, no friends, and no audience to help exonerate me. I found myself guilty to want to clean the streets against the will of those false sweepers.

My crime was to honour the real men and not the dirty, smelly ones. I was always on the other side of the lie and the demagogy. Some philosophers even dance with them and encourage them in their stupidity and in torturing the innocent and they promote them and applaud them.

It was a very moving experience in my life to the fact that I knew a real Prince, in ancestry and in heart. And even more, he is my friend and only my friend. Me! The miserable, stray dog which all his life was hunted and tracked down. My life is like a black, bottomless hole. I never tasted ripe fruit; my fruit were always sour, bitter or rotten. My bread was always stale. My water was lukewarm and salty. When the signs of hunger churn my stomach, because there is little else to churn inside it, I go hunting without a rifle, no harpoon and no arrows. These are the odds that I am up against. When I return, my hands are always bare, just like my heart and stomach. I return with empty bags, filled only with asparagus, olives and wild strawberries.

The game is always on the other side of the rapid, foaming river; it is always in the other field. Again my game keeps running from me every time I close in.

My luck smiled at me only once. Most likely out of pity more than anything else. While I was foraging in a wood one day, I met a donkey, very old and worn out by its long, productive life. Since then, my transport problem at least was sorted. But that poor donkey did not last that long. Its age was its illness, so there was no cure, it obliged him to stay in bed and I stayed by his side, nursing him until he died. I cried a lot because of the big loss. I took him and buried him under a big, olive tree old like himself. On the day of his funeral, there was only me, a few crows perched on the branch and also many tiny animals, ants, lizards and a number of insects. They made up his cortège.

Chiotby and I found ourselves in front of a big edifice for a building where that emblem stood towering over everything, its eyes, one open, one closed, with its opened eye on anyone that entered its territory. Chiotby told me a little about the history of the building.

"Dear friend, this venue is as old as dogs themselves. It is called The Eugah. It was named after its first ever judge. All the dogs of the entire world know of The Eugah. It is the tribunal of the most senior courts, where all crimes committed in the world by dogs are tried here. Occasionally crimes committed by other animals are admitted here too. Currently we are the only animals who possess a judiciary system, which is far more advanced and developed than the one of man. The court consists of three judges, only one of them deal with the trial and the other two each take a seat in the corners of the courtroom. Their job is to observe the judge for mistakes, if one should occur, then they intervene and have the power to replace him, all in order to ensure a fair trial. It is a bit similar to the lawyers too. The defendant is entitled to five lawyers, all of whom can fight his cause. However there is only one general prosecutor. And in case of his absence or death, he cannot be replaced and the trial continues without him or his substitute. I hope it is not too confusing for you, but you see that the defendant's defence is always stronger than his prosecution.

Also, witnesses are not needed to swear because dogs do not know how to lie, the witness statement is proof enough and nobody doubts it. Our judiciary system is not there to punish, but to correct and expose the ignorance of the ignorant and to educate others in the future. Like the old saying says, 'Ignorance does to the ignorant as the enemy does to its enemy.'

We provide rehabilitation for any dog found guilty. And once the rehabilitation is done, the dog moves on to be an exemplar citizen. And all those dogs that are present in the courtroom are rehabilitated and even manage to become better than the dogs that have never offended in their life before.

The expression guilty or not guilty, to us dogs we prefer to say 'blind or not blind'. You see now why our emblem of our justice has one eye open and the other closed. It is like ignorance next to the light," Chiotby explained to me the intricacy of their courts.

As soon as we stepped inside a huge copper door, we saw small sculptures of dogs smiling at the passer-bys. We found ourselves in what looked like a huge courtroom that spanned a thousand of hectares but we could still see the judge, sitting on a spectacular throne. We also saw the many staff behind us. There were benches all around him where hundreds if not thousands of dogs from all breeds were sitting and patiently waiting for this prestigious trial to begin. The only thing that this sight reminded me of was a huge stadium, however this one was contained in a very high enclosure. Here and there were German Shepherds circulating the courtroom. I assumed they were the official guards of the Eugah, they most prominent of their courts.

Chiotby remained loyal by my side without uttering a word. There was complete silence, spreading over the courtroom. All eyes were fixed on me. I was the strange animal to be tried today by the dogs. We slowly made our way towards the big throne were the judge was resting. The sky was illuminated without any light, where it got its source I did not know. I also noticed a few Ghoraab gliding over us.

Every dog was seated except for the select few of German Shepherds patrolling the room in groups of threes and smiling peacefully to the eager spectators. By now we were approximately one hundred yards away from the judges. My dear friend, Chiotby advanced and left me to take his place on the elevated podium and sat beside the judges. A group of guard dogs came and signalled for me to follow them.

I was lead to a small throne just right for my size. I was surprised at how comfortable it was. Strangely I felt at ease and a warm, strange sensation resided inside of me. The deafening silence prevailed over the courtroom, which gave the impression that nothing existed.

The judge was very old; he was a bulldog and was wearing a pair of looking glasses. They were suspended and were obstructed from falling by his upturned muzzle and low nostrils. The lines on his face looked like a thousand scars, it was like pieces of his face were glued together like in a jigsaw puzzle, all the signs of a long and productive life. It indicated the violence of before that no longer existed then, which time has put an end to. He had eyes typical to a judge, small, dark and sharp. When he looked at you, it was like arrows sent from his eyes to pierce the 'blind'. He possessed a big mouth, and his sharp, killer teeth that were planted on his jaw of steel were visible.

He scared me but impressed me at the same time. He moved slightly from time to time, but elegantly and to show his contempt for time wasting. On each of his sides, a white dog stood with a pile of white serviettes. From the first time I saw them I was racking my brain for what they could have possibly be used for. I soon learnt that they were to wipe the judge's dribble that continually seeped out of the judge's mouth involuntarily. And these dogs were there to wipe it.

On his head was an elaborate wig of ginger colour which was made from the mane of one lion, all the personnel in the courtroom also wore lion mane wigs but none as elaborate as the judge's. Only the Prince had different attire on, he still wore his beautifully illuminated crown, which distinguished him from all the rest.

You could have cut the atmosphere with a knife; it was so dense with tension. Everyone was waiting for the 'great event'.

To the side of me, I saw someone I did not expect to see, there was a female pig, very old too and very fat.

She was so large; her teats were dragging on the floor. She too was sitting on a small throne just like mine but was modified especially for her shape and size. Her throne looked more comfortable than mine. She arrived before me and I noticed that since I entered the packed courtroom, she did not avert her gaze away from me. I was slightly worried why I should provoke such a reaction from her, it seemed like she wanted to kill me with those eyes of hers.

During the long drawn silence I reassured myself by thinking, 'At least once in my life, I have come face-to-face with my judge, which is more than can be said for in my worldly life. He will judge me and question me and at last I will be able to respond and defend myself. And later we will see if I am blind or not blind.'

The blind is not blind as long as his light is preserved in his heart.

The same group of dogs came back once again and placed in front of me, olives, oranges and a jug of water and returned to their places. Only this time, I could not saviour anything, they were tasteless, and I think my taste buds were on revolt from the atmosphere around me. All of a sudden I heard the sound of a fanfare of trumpets, sharp at first then soft announcing the start of the trail.

The judge stood up, the two white dogs still wiping his neck and face. The audience all stood up too. I did the same but only the Prince remained seated. All the dogs then began to bark, all the dogs from all breeds. Do not falsely think it was a disagreeable sound, in my ears it sounded like a chorus of violins playing a sublime symphony which did not stop until Prince Chiotby stood up and gestured a sign of approval and for the barking to cease.

CHAPTER 10

THE TRIAL

The judge took his parole:

"My dear race, our dear Prince Chiotby and dear citizens, we are gathered here on the 23rd May 2050. We will begin a unique trial, a trial like no other, a trial that will be stamped on the memories of all canines for all time.

This is the first time in our history, in our kingdom that we are going to judge a human, this strange species which all of you know. We were living free and independent until his invasion in this world. Since that time, our life has been irreversibly changed forever and all the animals of the earth too. He is the cause of the extinction of many of our comrades; he exploited them, exterminated them, and even tamed them! This Man, this idiot stumbled one day on an idea to use anything to hide his physique, because he had a complex with his nakedness and since that day he thinks he is superior, why? He is different for a simple reason, he has clothes to hide his body and we do not.

Otherwise go and see him while he is asleep. He resembles a sack of rotten potatoes, smelly; he snores and lets out flatulence. His body inert like a dead body without being aware. It is idiocy in flesh and bones, when returning after a day at work, they look like bodies that are deaf, dumb and mute. We differ, as dogs we are proud, our dignity does not allow us to even wish to be like Man.

We know where he comes from, we know his origin. Trust me when I tell you that there is nothing to be proud of about that.

He begins in his mother's womb as small as a speck, then he is a piece of flesh, even the dingoes cannot find him appetising. At the embryonic stage, he resembles a tiny monster. This is the beginning of the monsters of the earth, they start as monsters and unfortunately die as monsters.

The Man is a monster disguised well by suits, hats, berets and so on and they smother themselves in perfumes to hide their body odours that all animals are born with."

It looks like this judge guessed my misery in pronouncing the date for the trial 23/05/50 that was very strange to say the least. Perhaps these dogs knew a lot more about me than I had originally thought, it was also the birthday of my little jewel, my daughter Miriam. And also of that ferocious wind which kept blowing at me without respite. The idea of celebrating this anniversary was so alien to me, to celebrate what though?

It is always the same wind, which I have known since the start of my existence. It ruins and destroys even the seas. It is a mad, blind, deaf and ferocious wind. My house ceased looking like a house. In its prime it was held up by six beams. The wind destroyed three of them and left the others to survive exposed to the elements. When I looked at a far corner behind the black flowers, a small beam was peeping out, frail and fragile, but at least it was propped up by another plank, a strong healthy one.

I started to clean them and stumbled on another two strong and healthy planks. I took them and embraced them strongly. I felt the sudden urge to name them; Faisal and the nice lank, Suraya.

I turned once again and I made something out moving in the dark. Yes, it was a hut supported by two beams, this time as if by magic. The hut followed me and its vision melted like everything else in this cruel world.

The judge was becoming more and more animated in describing without end, man and how he thought that he was immortal. I noticed that he only blamed man, he never mentioned the women. Perhaps he saw her as another on the list of unfortunate victims of man.

There was silence, the same great emptiness enveloping the court. The judge resumed his attack at man without respite after being refreshed by the silence. With his impressive voice reaching every corner of the room he said, "Since his apparition, all problems started, rabies was traced from the start of his existence. It was him that transmitted it to us. Before him we knew nothing of rabies, truant dogs and all other problems in life. He is the cause of all the pain. He believes himself to be more wise and superior, but he is simply an idiot, blind, deaf and mute.

His amusements are highly controversial; he creates wars for his own pleasure. He whiles away his time by killing one other. False heroes call themselves brave even in peace. But we know the extent of their bravery, when we run after them they scurry away like rabbits.

He is only courageous when he has a weapon in his hand and he becomes mad in shooting at everybody. He also creates courts to legitimise his crimes and idiocy; Hitler and Saddam and the list is long. The poor keep waiting for their Hitlers or their Saddams, and we only know when it is too late.

Hypocrisy and money are here to protect man, the vile monster. Man was created to destroy himself, and he is doing a fine job of it. He is blinded by his own desires. He is the volcano which consumes itself and all around it, in its crater and later it erupts and throws lava violently which kills and burns. He is only here to kill and burn anything that moves.

He is also like the dormant volcano that is tranquil for years but then kills by vengeance without reason. He is that fire which only burns not the one that warms. He is the rattlesnake, which keeps guard, waiting for anything that moves. He is the vulture that flies at low altitude looking for its prey that is going onto dead or the already dead. He is the rat that swims in the sewers and does not care to learn anything. He is the black spider weaving its web without end to trap to kill. If he manages to transform himself into another animal, he will certainly be a sick donkey, deaf and blind. And the worst is that he thinks he is the most smart and superior of all creatures! How ridiculous does that sound?

How can we explain that he is nothing? All we need to do is just wait and see him going to his tomb, and turn into dust like everything else. When he enters his tomb he will be good for only one thing, being nourishment for those poor worms that will consume him without knowing it is human flesh. Then he will no longer be the handsome man. He will merely be a few pounds of smelly, blue and green flesh, exposed to those worms eating him peacefully. He, who created perfumes and wore, them all the time. He walks imitating the kings and ate like the kings and spoke like the kings. However this façade will not last forever, just wait with patience and we will see him without doubt transformed into the most horrible image."

The judge concluded his amazingly accurate perceptions of us; I was undecided to whether I should recoil back in shame or to shout slogans at him of support. It was truly amazing to hear another animal's opinions of us and the judge seemed to be very learned of us. But it seemed his vehemence for us was not abated, he turned to address me, his eyes were like arrows piercing me, and

THE VERDICT

I dared not flinch. I became petrified and stupefied like an idiot staring at him...I braced myself, "You! The man, the bloodstained idiot, you create hurt by your virtues and arrogance. And all those laws you created to launder your crime and destroy others. Everything you want and hope to have, you call it desire. And it is your desire, which dictates your laws, and through those laws you burn not only yourselves but also others. Since your invasion to this world you only do what I have already mentioned. We are very far from being impressed, by your toys and gadgets. You invent them because you are bored in this world and you get easily bored because you are imbeciles. You are good for nothing! You created telephones, yes, televisions, cars, computers without knowing you are speeding the rate of your destruction and exterminations, no more no less. Your progress is only material, you call it improvement and progress. What improvement exactly and what progress? This 'so-called' progress is fit for imbeciles.

Social issues? Moral issues? You keep digging a deeper hole, which your ancestors started. You are always digging that horrible black hole not knowing where you are going. And if we say to you stop, this big mistake of digging up holes, come out and see the sun which shines and waits for you. You gallop in frenzy and you start shouting at us by holding your slogans, 'We only follow our ancestors'.

You do not realise that you are the worst species of all creatures. You transgress, men with men, women with women, some even with kids, some with dogs, cats, donkeys, you are not fussy, anything that moves really will do.

And what about those foetuses that we find thrown away in bins by their parents. That is a true demonstration of your heart and virtues. And when we think about this foetus, you despise it and claim that one day you will rule the world. This world is disintegrating more and more as it turns on itself. We know that this world is turning on its axis and descending lower and lower drifting away from the sun.

It is idiocy and mediocrity of this man, which tires him and adds to his world any of its value. Do not attempt to talk about your ingenuity, it is us who are the sole possessors.

You are a chameleon, constantly changing your colour; we still do not know your true colour. Man cheats everyone, beginning with himself. He is what he is today, because he was carved by his law more than the virtues and principles which should rightly sculpt an individual.

It ceases to amaze me that you call this carnage and your immoralities; desires, passions, love and freedom. You create wars to liberate people but you imprison them only to liberate them later, a very cunning game. Their happiness is short lived as you imprison again to release them again. This pattern is what is more commonly known as revolutions. And we are witnessing those idiocies, which you repeat again the same chorus since your creation. You are useful for one thing, creating fire and fuelling it by stirring it with the poker.

My mind is set, man is mad and his madness is his blindness. He assumes he sees and he does not know he is blind because he never knew the light.

However, his plight in this world is to search for that light, but he is caught in a vicious circus because his hypocrisy and arrogance make him blind on this journey. He walks and stumbles without the steady support of a cane to guide him as his only companion is his false virtues and desires which guide him through his muddy path to add to his filth.

I am certain this universe will be more beautiful and interesting without his presence."

And here the judge took a pause and was still standing up, watching me always. His gaze, so severe was killing me more than his sharp words; as the evidence were been stacked against me. I did not feel any fear, foolishly perhaps, but on the contrary I felt a great release through my body.

I felt like that poor woman who has just given birth, her child separated form her warm, supporting body and lived through it by the skin of her teeth. She is watching the strange child beside her, he is crying. How appropriate to begin this world in that tone. She knows what will await him in this cruel world.

Man is his own enemy; he is mad and is the cause for his insanity.

From where I was sitting, I could see my friend, Prince Chiotby gesturing to me and I understood what he wanted to say, "Don't be scared, I am on your side!" The judge sat down, the same barking broke out again, soft and melodious as before... no, better. This lasted for a good few moments until Chiotby signed majestically for its end. The whole court plunged into silence. There I took the opportunity to let my mind wonder as well as my sensations, which took me where nobody went on even in adventures.

No wind, no storm, the view was very clear and serene. I found myself climbing on a roof of a beautiful star, beaming with light. And from this height I am looking down on earth, that small sphere, the pip in the fruit, all the pain and problems orbiting it exercising total confusion. It was only later we knew it is us that orbit the sun, not the other way around.

The sun is here to observe us during the day; the light there is fixed, waiting for us to go towards it like moths. This world or rather this old driftwood from an old wreck thrown in the universe. The big universe makes us scared. This vast space, which I keep contemplating night and day without courage to approach or touch it. That big mass hesitating, not knowing where to go. The man is pressing on its brakes and disturbs it in playing games. He is the clown who performs his habitual tricks. He sings, dances, grimaces and performs his myth. Yes, I see that driftwood lost in the intense greatness. That driftwood for man which is nothing, but when I see this heart, which dictates and takes us sometimes beyond the universe, all of a sudden I see myself larger until I touch the sun and sky and I become its light.

The silence is still there like a white rock covering the entire court, witnessing the great discipline and the wisdom of all those dogs around me. The judge stood up and took control of the speech.

"Your highness, the Prince, my dear brothers and sisters, I declare the trial is to open."

It was what we were waiting for but it only made the silence more audible. Nobody stirred, like life was brought to a sudden stop in the courtroom. A group of German shepherd's headed towards the pig, they saluted and helped her rise, that pig was so old that she needed their help.

They began to carefully place each of her teats in a cotton basket, she had twenty bulging teats, massive and swollen, they lifted them all before they placed a stretcher under her, the logistic operation went so smoothly we did not hear any noise, even the pig seemed like she did not feel the movement. They lifted her onto a chariot, covered in white flowers and flashing fairy lights. They helped illuminate her features. Once finished, I could tell she was laying comfortably but all the comfort in the world would not subdue her gaze, she still stared at me like she had intentions of murdering me, her face had war declared on it.

The judge broke the silence, "Mr. Man you behold that in front of you is Madame Pigiotte, the plaintiff who has laid down accusations against you of the most heinous nature, namely that you killed and massacred her twenty babies, their names; Piga, Pigb, Pigc, Pigd, Pige, Pigf, Pigg, Pigh, Pigi, Pigj, Pigk, Pigl, Pigm, Pign, Pigo, Pigp, Pigq, Pigr, Pigs and Pigt. They were brutally murdered by you in a farm in Hainault, in Barkingside, London. Dear accused I pass over to Madame Pigiotte in the witness stand who will attempt to recount the events that took place on that dreadful day 01/ 04/ 50, be at ease no need to rise."

Madame Pigiotte started crying uncontrollably. The same guards that assisted her ran to wipe away her abundant tears; they began to gush out of her eyes like water gushing out of a pressure hose. The dogs were still trying to control her flow of tears; they even reached my toes as I felt the warmth of the saline puddles. It was pitiful; I could not help but join her in grieving for her unimaginable loss. Amidst her crying and her snorts she managed to compose herself enough to say, "Your honour the judge, ladies and gentlemen, dogs of the court, I thank you all from the bottom of my heart that you are all present here today to give me this opportunity to avenge the death of my children."

She paused to cry again, "As you see I am very old, my husband was already dead before the death of my glorious children. I remained miserably widowed and nobody wanted to marry me, firstly because of the baggage twenty children brings and I am not being modest when I say I am not attractive any more.

All I had were my children, the last legacy of my dear husband, they reminded me of my husband, I loved him madly. We were both very young when we met each other, it was springtime, and I used to live on a different farm to my dear Pigio. It was love at first sight! After a short and intense courtship we married. We tried to have children but we only became pregnant in our old age, they very year that I became pregnant, Pigio died from a heart attack and after a few months I gave birth to twenty healthy piglets. Everyone from nearby farms were envious of my beautiful babies. They had blue eyes and prominent snouts just like you dog's. Everyone told me that they were a rare species. My children were very happy, bouncy kids. Pigio's parents used to come to visit from time to time; you see they were the proudest grandparents alive. I was in bliss, Pigio was a marvellous husband, he was also serving my invalid mother who was staying with us. She was blind and I was her only child. Pigio looked after me and my mother. My mother died two years before Pigio's heart attack. I lived a happy life but from his untimely death my problems have been mounting.

I remember it was roughly four o'clock in the afternoon, I only remember because it was teatime. This man who stands in front of you, this 'monster' that you call Mr. Man stormed into our barn with three of his friends all equally ruthless and all very drunk. They were very boisterous, drinking, dancing, singing and more drinking. I was very near to them and was minding my own business; I was nursing my children before sending them to bed, for they were very sleepy because we woke up very early that day as all days.

Pigo woke up, he was the most attentive, and he probably tasted the fear in my milk. I started to kiss him and assure him and comfort him. He was my favourite because he looked very much like his dad. I started caressing him as all proper mothers aught to do. Then I saw this murderer pointing and laughing at us. I understood straight away that their fun had not been all got; they wanted to do something sinister to my babies and me. The children were drinking their milk as I already mentioned, the sucking made them sleepy apart from Pigo who was in my arms. I started to fear for their safety. After an hour, at about five this monster and his gang headed towards us still dancing and singing. The oldest of the gang tumbled and fell down on me, I felt like biting him but I resisted as to not disturb my babies in their innocent sleep and peaceful meal.

His friends lifted him up and plonked him on the table. He was very drunk and seemed unaware of everything, however them! They mistook the fall as being my fault, they pounced on us savagely. They tore my children from my teats, the milk from their tiny mouths poured on me. I tried to fight back for them to stop, but they were stronger than me. I was chained, I became hysterical, I screamed and pulled at my hair. The kids called out to me for help, 'Mummy, Mummy, Mummy!

Save us..." she paused to swallow her tears, "Save us! They want to kill us' I was pulling at the chain; it was too strong for me though. You see if you are a parent then you will know how pathetic and hopeless I felt. I kept shouting to block out my babies screams, I was biting myself so that I was feeling pain too.

One of the three men kicked me in my mouth and cut my screams short. Blood gushed from everywhere, from my snout and ears. My breasts were all bloody, my body in a pool of blood.

I was paralysed, all I could do was pray and witness the most atrocious scene in my life. Watching my children stepping away from my life slowly slaughtered and butchered into pieces. I was overcome and fainted. I forced myself to stay awake with the hope of saving my babies. But this monster and his friends were very quick. I knew when they slaughtered the last because I could not hear their screams of 'mummy' their pink blood and innocence spread on the floor.

The men were dancing in the blood; they opened more bottles of wine and started again with their act. They returned to the table where my slaughtered children lay lifeless. They each had a sabre and finished the massacre by decapitating them. They started to sever their heads and throw them on the floor. After that, they started cutting their bodies into tiny pieces, I fainted again, but I fought the urge, the only strength left in me was the fake hope that only mothers possess. I saw their limbs moving slightly as if life was still in them. For a split second I thought my kids were not yet dead!

I begged the men to stop and leave them again by imploring, 'they haven't finished their milk yet'. I shouted and screamed. Nothing made a difference to their calloused hearts.

The worst was still to come; the old one woke from his drunken stupor. He woke up with an appetite and asked for my babies hearts as a delicacy because he adored barbecued pigs' hearts. They were only too happy to rip their hearts out and put them in a blue container. I could see twenty hearts, my twenty treasures, and my twenty pearls swimming in blood.

He staggered on the bowl then this monster grabbed the first heart he could at random, I recognised it, it was Pigo's heart, all pink and unblemished. It was like I was seeing my dear Pigio's too. Here I could no longer support the scene. 'Please, I beg you, especially that heart!!' they were too drunk to hear my cries. The old one took the sabre and used it as a skewer, he filled it with the hearts and placed it on the fire. I heard their hearts sizzling in the fire. They did not know that my heart to was in that fire too and I fainted again into a coma.

It was until the next day that I woke up. All that was left of my children where bones scattered everywhere on red stained soil of the barn. The dogs cried tears of sympathy for me when I cried," she began to exhibit signs of physical pain for the first time as well as emotional. The judge asked her to continue politely.

"Your honour, I cannot find the words to describe my pain. As you see my breasts are still lactating because they do not know that my children have died. My heart also has not for one minute ceased in its grief. It swallows my heart and my being. You have certainly noticed my physique, it suffers and my weight has surpassed the norms expected of my race. I am a sick, old pig."

The poor Madame Pigiotte described her pains, her sadness and calamities. She moved the whole court, not one dog did not cry. Quite suddenly Madame Pigiotte began to stir from pain, she began to stretch and shake uncontrollably. Under the many layers of fat you could see her heart beat rapidly wanting to break free from her chest. Her body began to fit, like she is about to give birth. The guards rushed to her sides to comfort her and try to understand the reason for the sudden change. They spoke softly trying to calm her, but she did not respond. Her eyes opened and were fixed on something very far. With her eyes wide open, her body convulsing, we heard a huge explosion like a rap on a big drum or a clap of thunder. All the dogs barked in a confused chorus. The sound came from the teats deflating. The milk splashed everywhere. The judge, Prince, Jury all were painted in white with her milk. Panic spread across the court, The Eugah. The milk flew at me and drenched my face. I felt its warmth but it was swiftly followed by its bitter after-taste.

Madame Pigiotte was tossing and turning in agony, then there was peace, fatal peace where her soul returned to its final resting place. Her body lay calm and inert. From the middle of her chest was an opening, her heart came out of her chest, it was still beating its last faint beat like an old grandfather clock, it couldn't keep up with the pace of life and stopped forever.

It was in these unhappy circumstances that the tragedy of Madame Pigiotte came to an end. She died with her bitter milk, breasts deflated, her heart ejected.

A team of dogs promptly started to lap up all the milk. Within a fraction of a second, the court resumed its spotless gleam, like nothing happened there at all. They covered Madame Pigiotte with a black shroud studded with black flowers that emitted a sad, monotone perfume. They carried her out of the court and already there was a cortège mourning her. The peace in the court was disturbed and there was great movement, except for me of course, I became the spectator instead. I became aware of new faces, which replaced the former faces of the court. The judge remained the same all but for a change in his uniform. He was wearing a fine black robe and the same magnificent wig. The court was adjourned, but I knew they were preparing to continue with the trial, they had already lost too much precious time by the sudden death of Madame Pigiotte. The silence returned once more to the court, the judge was the first to break it as usual.

"We are very touched by this sudden loss of Madame Pigiotte and also by the death of her children and may they rest in peace. Mr Man you have heard all the accusations regarding those unimaginable crimes that you committed, I now give you a chance to defend yourself, should you wish so?"

"Your honour, I too am touched also of all the pain and suffering that Madame Pigiotte has had to endure. As a human being I can testify that I too am witness to the atrocities man has committed since his creation. He is cannibalistic by nature. Your Honour I swear I am not guilty...I mean not blind of this genocide and these hideous crimes. I wished that the late Madame Pigiotte were still alive to tell her in front of the court that I am innocent, and I will prove it to the court. I do not even eat pig because I have certain principles in my life, which I uphold. Pigs, if only there were a lot more people like me then the world will overpopulate your Honour.

I admit, I do live in Hainault, and quite close to the farm but I did not carry out this carnage of slaughtering those twenty hearts, those twenty 'pearls' as their mum referred to them. No, your Honour, my life was too miserable to kill those poor innocent pigs and their mother. I say it, and say it again.... I plead not blind!" I said all this with hardly taking a breath, I conveyed the truth as best I could, and the set-up of the court was not something I knew of.

This judge at least seamed to be thoughtful to what I had to say. He turned to the Prince for the first time since the trial, like he was asking him for his advice, all done by an exchange of a few glances. The court adjourned, there was a shuffle of seats, and then the personnel surrounded the Prince to deliberate my future.

After half an hour they returned to their positions. The judge stood up and I braced myself for the verdict, "Mr. Man concerning the genocide towards the children of Madame Pigiotte we feel there was not sufficient proof or evidence to place you at the scene of the crime. We find you…not blind!"

I somehow felt safe at the hands of these animals, I was cleared, the truth prevailed at last…Amidst the excitement the verdict brought, no body noticed my dear friend, the Prince steal away from his throne straight towards me. After a quick embrace he quietly whispered to me, "Dear friend, this is not the end for you, there is yet another test regarding the affair of the Koreans," then with the same speed and agility he returned to his throne, leaving me wide-mouthed. Not again surely? Another story, one of which I had no idea about.

The judge resumed his position. It was met by the barking of dogs which tore up the silence that the judge's movement brought to the courtroom. I began to see lights in the ceilings. There was silence again.

He stood up and with renewed strength he said, "Mr. Man, this time the allegations have come directly from the kingdom of dogs," my heart sank, perhaps they will not be so understanding against their own kind, "that you consumed the flesh of dogs and have created a flourishing industry where our meat is sold. You are of Korean Citizenship and you come from the province Gwangmyeong 250 miles from the capital Seoul. You employ 2000 staff to exercise this criminal activity.

And furthermore we all know that you eat your own flesh sometimes and now you are to exterminate us...

Mr. Chiennard is with us today and is the sole survivor of his tribe. He tells of males, females, even pups that were all slaughtered and then eaten by man. Mr. Chiennard perhaps you would care to elaborate further?" the judge sat down and I had to bear more fresh allegations by plaintiffs I had never crossed during my life.

Mr. Chiennard spoke proudly with a confidence that Madame Pigiotte lacked, perhaps this time I would not be let-off so swiftly? "Your Highness, the exalted Prince and your Honour, dear brothers and sisters, I am from Korea, a land so blissful and peaceful you cannot imagine. My family have lived there since before the arrival of the first man, before his rude intrusion life was peaceful as I said and prosperous, but it soon began to change. Nobody knows the cause of the brutal change, but I can certainly make an informed guess! All our compatriots began to worry for their lives and so naturally began to flee those regions, whose borders were not as secure as they are now. I myself, had to battle 1001 dangers to be here with you today! Every time I crossed a new country, no body knew that I was a fugitive, it was certainly an advantage to be a dog otherwise I would have been hung by man.

During my life, I witnessed a whole spectrum of colours of problems, especially crossing borders. I saw humans kill each other at the border. But me, I was crossing like I had a thousand passports. Your Honour, they are insane, our race is in danger especially in the regions where I came from. We keep seeing more and more slaughter houses being built…one every five minutes. You see, over there our flesh is a delicacy; the human beings prefer our meat over others. They find it is succulent. They make hot dogs, and not one butcher does not have us on display in his counter. They use everything, heads, guts…. it is horrible. They are assassinating us as we speak and have almost exterminated us.

The worst is some find our private parts the most succulent part of our body.

Your Honour do not trust this man any more. We must stop him, cure him. He is crazy and insane. This is an ongoing problem that our dear brothers are facing and the danger looms day and night." he seemed slightly agitated by the judges interruption, it seemed to him that the judge was the one that asked him to elaborate, and as far as he was concerned he was just warming up.

"Thank you very much Mr. Chiennard. The matter is indeed very grave. If this disease of acquiring taste for our meat would spread across the world, then our race will be erased from the face of the Earth. Ultimately man is destroying himself at the same time, it is his loss too. Is it not better to put you under surveillance, to control you and you become our servant? Then maybe you will forget this fake attitude, arrogance that you are masters of the universe. Rest assured that you would be given all your rights from the start. We will chain you and then at least you will not kill each other and ultimately create those false wars of yours. Tell us the truth, once in your life, what do you want? We can help and get you out of your dead-end lives and your craziness. You cannot carry on unassisted; we have seen that you are all blind, deaf and mute. Dear Chiennard, all that you have said is reiterated, we saw a shocking documentary broadcasted by the BBC that laid out footage to support your claims. We were all utterly shocked at the capacity for the man cruelty, among the disturbing footage, we even saw dogs being skinned alive!" As the judge said these last words, his awful gaze fell down on me again, it signalled for me to talk.

"Your Honour, gentlemen of the court, Mr. Chiennard I plead not blind! You can see clearly that I am not remotely from the parts that Mr. Chiennard speaks of. I am not Korean, I am black and I come from Africa. My eyes are not slanted and I do not look Chinese. Physically

I do not resemble someone from there and in sentiments too I do not resemble them.

I was a wanderer in my life, I roamed Africa for a period of time, and then I was obliged to leave. The fire that forced me to leave was so fierce that the flames and smoke have not yet been able to be extinguished.

Did I say I come from North Africa? No, I am not so sure now, from North, South, East or West, it is all a blur. Those compass points are useless, they should be there to navigate you away from where misery is coming from and where it is heading. I come from the centre where the four points meet and also where the wars are created.

I see myself black, and am proud to be, and I say it openly, my skin colour harmonises with what I feel inside with my deception and problems. Being blue, white, black and yellow does not matter, misery has only one colour, and when it strikes it brands and disfigures, paralyses, smites your tongue and handicaps you for all eternity. Yes, I admit I am a man as you have knick-named me. All that you have attributed to my race, I not only agree with, but confirm that it is true.

I came with my dear friend the Prince Chiotby to discover your world, this kingdom of yours. I will tell you the truth; I would rather belong to your world. The man who I am, this nightmare is the nightmare which haunts and prosecutes me.

I will do everything and will comply with all your laws. Do not accuse me of the crimes I did not commit, of course I represent this species of human beings, but it has been a long time since I have rejected the lowliness of their hypocrisy and greed for gold. Gold has the power to transform kings, princes, presidents of state and their valets into servants and dishonourable human beings.

It does not matter if I am a dog, rat, bat or ant, I will always be me, and I have pride of existence without the evilness of man. I will never change what I have in my heart for all the treasures in the universe. In fact the whole universe rotates around me and my heart. Without my heart, the universe will not exist. Non existence is far better than existing without my heart.

Your Honour, my heart bleeds black, bitter blood, my heart bears a resemblance to the beautiful heart of Madam Pigiotte.

I ran away from my kind to look for a better one, cleaner than water and snow. My travels were always full of danger. I was like those pioneers of gold, risking their lives, but my gold is different to the gold we find on this Earth. *My* gold is in my heart. All this I discovered when I was star-gazing. Since that time my gold shines without end, hunting the evil.

I ran away from my race for a better world like yours. I would like to integrate and live among you."

I kept quiet; I could not find any more words. My tears took their cue, streams running down my cheeks. I think I was conscious when I told the dogs that I wished to join them and for them to accept me, so that my dear friend Chiotby will always stay by my side.

I lifted my head and all eyes were upon me, my friend was weeping and in unison all of the other dogs were weeping too, weeping at my pitiable state. Small streams of tears began to form on the ground. The prince Chiotby came down from his throne, headed straight towards me, still crying, he kissed and embraced me. The collective cries made a soft gloomy hum which was rising. It was a soft wind that can move flowers and even trees without breaking them.

Chiotby and I were still locked in our embrace; he tore himself away and along with the judges, deliberated over my fate. There was silence, which raised my doubts; I was in a state of confusion, not knowing what was to become of me. Was I going to be turned into a dog or to remain a man?

Two different worlds, two different species two different ways of thinking.

"Dear friend Adam, being here, I Prince Chiotby, represent this glorious kingdom and the court, I have great pleasure to declare the defendant 'Not Blind', and also that we accept you as a member of our community. We of course will need to impose certain conditions which I will specify later."

I was relieved that my dream had been fulfilled and that my suffering was going to be halted. I will be able to live happily ever after. Without controlling myself I began to jump with joy, it had been the first time in my life that I was pronounced innocent. However I will never be able to enjoy my innocence because I know wherever else I go, they will find me guilty, guilty only of innocence.

At least that court of dogs gave me my innocence, my natural born right, even though by that time it had been battered and bruised for a long time.

I lifted my arms not to surrender but to declare, "Long live the dogs, long live the dogs, and long live the dogs, down with man, with evil, with cruelty and stench!" and with an action that even surprised me, my mouth opened and a deep, gruff sound came out. I was barking! All the dogs soon barked in chorus. I was in either pure ecstasy or utter delirium. In either case a joy I have never felt and will never be replicated in the whole kingdom.

The whole court became illumined and amazingly took on a completely different image. It was not recognisable any more; even the Eugah logo was removed. I must have left the courtroom a defendant and entered a beautiful garden cleared of any accusation, but how? This change seemed to take place in a split second.

This garden was very vast; flowers that were lights lined it. I knew that this was the celebration of my initiation into the race of canines. All the dogs accepted me like I was one of their own. I was no longer that man, that stranger, that illegal.

The Prince, jubilant, ran towards me and said, "dear friend, I offer my congratulations. From now on you are a dog like us, you belong to our dear race. Our friendship is galvanised and is transformed into brotherhood, like when silver is transformed into gold, the only worthy upgrade. I was very happy since the start of our epic odyssey, a unique journey, and its first in history. Dear brother, the kingdom of the dogs offer you a gift in proving our sincerity and love for our brotherhood. We propose to you to marry one of us."

And there my joy doubled twofold to know that I was going to marry a bitch, but which bitch was going to accept a former man as a husband. We will see later.

The prince continued, "My dear brother, it is the judge himself that is offering you his daughter, who comes from Alaska. She is very beautiful; she is blond with green eyes. She has golden fur, which looks and feels like silk. She is both young and intelligent, and strong and big. Her name is Pearla, she is my little sister. Obviously I would like to know your opinion. If you desire to marry her because the judge, or rather my father is waiting with her for our attendance."

I did not need time think, "Of course I accept, it is a great honour to marry a bitch, and furthermore…a princess!"

I became thoughtful and daydreamed briefly, that I will become a Prince in my turn. I said, "YES," without adding any comment.

We left together the Prince and the future Prince hand in paw. I attempted to walk like a Prince, I needed to practice, I was nearing my future bride and I became very nervous. As we approached I could already see that Pearla was even more beautiful than her brother led me to believe. She was indeed very beautiful, very imposing, with all the right attributes you associate with a princess. I could not help but be impressed, she stood tall and majestic. She was seated serenely inside a circle of delicate flowers, letting out an intoxicating beautiful smell. The Prince very briefly fabricated a picture of me; described me briefly to her in saying, "My dear sister Pearla, you have in front of you, a man who is a man no more, indeed the most beautiful of his race."

I felt touched at the high esteem he held me in, he then came to me and whispered to me, "My friend what do you think, she is beautiful, is she not?"

I responded very quietly without her hearing me, "I do see in front of me, the most beautiful lady I have ever set my eyes on." by her sight only, I could tell she wanted to say many things. Her face was like the sun, expressing, happiness, love and all her virtues. The Prince, after his short introduction of me, told her that her future happiness was only ever to be assured in an alliance with me. He left her, and both father and son left us.

As soon as they left, my confidence deserted me; I started shaking in every part of my body. After wanting to say something, I felt obliged to say anything, but I was worried if I should stutter to the extent that my lips started to tremble. I at least had the courage to stand up, I put one foot in front of the other, and unintentionally,

I was pacing around her. Pearla, the princess did not say anything, but her eyes did not let me go at all since the start of my stupid show. Tired and deceived I went back to her and sat down in front of her still shaking...

"Mr. Man, can I inquire to why you are shaking and circling me?" Pearla asked me in her smooth voice.

"My dear princess," I responded, "trembling is an instinct in us when we lay eyes on such beautiful wives, like you and about pacing around you, I just wanted to make sure you are the wife of my dreams...I think...I find you very beautiful, I will venture to say that you are even more beautiful than me. I will confess and I accept our marriage without knowing more about you. I can already see great happiness paved our way and many children will come out of our union. You are young and beautiful and I will strive to make you happy all my life," I continued to express what I felt towards her, and the sincerity of the love I felt. She remained ever quiet, listening to me attentively.

Her only response was the lowering of her gaze every now and then. The jade colour of her eyes unlocked the secret of her beauty. She was dazzling! Once I conveyed what I felt and what I was feeling, I stopped and waited for her encouraging words.

She spoke, her voice radiated warmth, and it was smooth and sorceress like black magic. Her voice was like notes of music swaying in the air. I did not want to her to stop speaking.

THE VERDICT

"Mr. Man I have to tell you the truth, and in doing so, perhaps I will hurt you without aiming to. It is preferable that I hurt you now and not later. I also have my father and brother to think of, I do not wish to upset them by refusing you. When we speak of happiness we must begin with sincerity, especially when you are in the pursuit of happiness. Likewise, misery is created when happiness is lacking. Mr. Man I can never accept to be the wife of a man. I can readily marry outside my race to a rat, bat, or even a fox who we despise so much, rather than marry a man! Even our contempt to the fox cannot negate any matrimonial alliance between us, but marrying a man.... but you do not even have a tail! I find that too strange, I find *you* strange, you walk on two hind legs and we walk on four. You have no shame, your body is naked with very little hair or fur. Must I list all your faults? The list is very long. And it is these faults, which induce me from approaching you. In short, I find you very unattractive. I could hide my contempt for you, though with difficulty by not saying a word, and proclaim my mad fondness of you. But then what will we gain, a very short and unhappy marriage followed by a divorce? Certainly you will appreciate my frankness," she said confidently, defiantly but with the subtly only she could bring to words so harsh.

She became more and more lovely in my eyes. She kept enchanting me, I understood the manifestation of my trembles towards her were present in fear of rejection, and this sense of foreboding meant one thing, sooner or later my dream will end. Unlike other endings, this ending was very sad for me, that beautiful Princess refused to cement my happiness; for once in my life *I* could have been happy. So here, my journey ended, ended with a truth that brought my enchanting dream to an abrupt ending, "A bitch refused a man!".

The man is me and you! We have to stop lying to ourselves. When do we realise that man does not impress others any more. The biggest error that man has made since the beginning of his time is that he does not see himself as others creatures see him. And the cursed mirror which is supposed to show us a true reflection of ourselves does not help, it shows us a contorted image instead.

I knew of a mirror in an old wardrobe in Alicante, Spain, which made the onlooker seem taller. And I saw hoards of people all short and stocky cue to only take a glimpse of themselves to enjoy the false allure....

Pearla, the beautiful stood up and waved graciously and left me forever, still her eyes downcast. Her departure brought my friend's arrival, I could tell he was sad at the news his sister conveyed to him but he was still sporting a smile. I explained my defeat of my heart. And my distress, which ended. The Prince cried, he hugged me strongly, he bid me farewell and ran off, flying out the way we flew in, he took off to other horizons and unlike other people in their dream state I knew that this was the end of my dream, "Goodbye dear Prince, goodbye dear Princess!"

I fell off my bed with a loud THUD!

I woke up dazed like I was far away. I was an intruder to the man's world, which was frightening and filthy.

I am the veteran soldier who is struck off the fighting list without a sabre or bow. I am heading towards other fronts, I jump on the enemy willed at death and all of a sudden I find myself besieged by all those verdicts

THE VERDICT OF 30 APRIL 2007
IT WAS 12PM

Today, it is not Sunday but it will nevertheless be a day that will surely bleed my heart dry. I was in a constant state of alert. I have been hunted all my life without any respite. I do not know why it is though, is that the instinct of animals or the effect of those strong and cruel illusions? I find myself in this empty dream without any light, ultimately in a false dream. All of a sudden I was beckoned to reality with pinching sensations all around my body. I resisted in pretending not to feel anything. And I did not want this dream to end, not for all the money in the world.

It was six in the evening, and the first signs of the storm. Braving the wind and rain, I planted twenty freesias in my garden. They were red and yellow. I planted them and watered them with hope to protect them from the wind. I will only know later the fruit of my labours.

This time I can say in my turn; this is life, I felt tightness in my heart and also I felt my hands and feet tied together like I was mummified. Then a searing heat followed by an enormous noise like the crunching of a castle of glass. I fell down and ultimately back to this dirty world again.

This was the 21st April 2007. It was nine in the morning exactly, I was in the eye of the storm, everything burned and boiled, and everything reduced to nothing. It was a nightmare while I was still awake. It was like a Tsunami of me, which took me to a deep abyss. I had no choice, I let myself go. I was fighting back and had to claw onto anything I could.

The thousands of currents teamed against me, I lost my orientation and did not know where I was. It was most likely the end of my world, which will be a huge relief from the pain. All looked like a tornado, which spun at high velocity, that I could not see anything, all was black. I was at the mercy of my bitterness, which had free reign to do as it wished with me. It was not my choice, it was my life and I had to grab onto anything I could. And my tears could help, you could barely distinguish them as they were mixed with the waves, everything immersed in absolute black.

Oh my God! I touched something soft and fragile and with a scent that I could recognise among hundreds of perfumes of the world. Yes, it was she, my soul galloping to rescue me. It loosened my ties, she pulled me towards her and wiped away my tears and heart. She lifted me up and took me with her. Once again she delivered me from safety, and caressed me to sleep.

Since the beginning of this verdict, time with its hands was tearing me by every minute and second. Today it is 27th April 2007 and still no news. I languish and my stress keeps prolonging. I forget the verdict; it only exists in my dreams. But my dream is being cut sometimes, like a spasm, agonising in trying to be completed in peace. The seconds become years, and minutes become centuries. I see that this day is dying and taking with it any hope left.

And me, I cry here and there for a love I have been denied for three centuries. My whole body cries and nobody is here to console me, I have only myself and my dear Chiotby to survive and wait for the verdict which makes me survive or transform my dreams into nightmares.

I went back to my journey of dreams, holding onto the last shreds of hope for the 30/04/07. But that bitterness took over me and ordered me to place down my quill. I was simply too sad to write, too sad to even dream.

Today was the 30/04/07 and tomorrow will be 01/05/07.

It has arrived, the day of the dreaded verdict. It was midday, they pronounced the verdict. I was found guilty of my innocence once again I felt a fever which enveloped all my body. My body was in rebellion to that jury with their mindless conscience that hurt me so much. They were done; they did their work, job done. Was it sorted out though?

THE VERDICT

That evening the judge and the jury went back to their homes, to celebrate their masterpiece in having a nice dinner with their families and watching TV and they will see themselves as heroes of the day.

They condemned me in finding me guilty...of what? My only crime is my innocence, which lives with me day and night. But tonight I cry, I will not eat; I will not watch TV because I am the guilty one. My heart once solid has been burnt to cinders, its valves, aortas demolished by the verdict. They killed me whilst still alive. I see myself a blur like being in a train that surpasses the speed of light. I cannot read the names of the stations or stops or to read the faces of people. Also I have no idea where I am to go next in this new chapter of my life.

The following day life outside my bubble was in normal running order; the sun was beautiful and majestic. But only to others, I could only see a black round hole. My world has become obscured by the verdict, which cut me into a thousand pieces and makes me older within the space of forty minutes

I tried to cry, but my body would not oblige at all. It was too hurt and torn to connect the right action with the right emotion. In order to put my body in its right place, my tears bled within me. It is perhaps that side of life, hard or toilsome, that many people do not understand and so therefore put an end to their lives. I will go further and deepen myself, I wring my heart with my hands and I watch the sky and I implore the light, which illuminates and gives life and warmth to anything that exists or touches.

The sun, the stars and all souls. And from there comes the existence of all stars, the sun and soul. That is my foothold to defy this disfigured world. I jump out of the train and tear apart from its shear power. Nothing scares me as long as that light is there to save me. A few seconds more, or a few years more, I will go and will enter my grave, which eagerly waits for me somewhere, I do not know where. My tomb is only a walk-in passage; I enter from one side, and can exit at the other. Once again and so I can sleep, I might faint along the way, I can enter a state of coma but I will never die to perish.

Personally, I do not care about my corpse especially now, I keep ageing and I do not like my body any more. It makes me feel tired and it imprisons me with it. I cannot walk with it like before; it forces me to sit down and sometimes forces me to stay in bed to nurse it. Whereas before it used to carry out my physical demands, it now does the opposite.

I prefer my soul to my body. She never sleeps she is always exploiting new horizons.

Today is the 01/05/07 and the sun once again is beautiful and majestic but I will defeat it. And I see it obscured, from now on; the whole world has been transformed by the verdict. Pronounced by the very man who I reject my association with.

THE VERDICT

And after two days another verdict, parallel to ours came and hit that family, the married millionaire with his child. They all died on the spot. The millionaire, his son, his best friend and the pilot. It was a hard impact for their family and they were crying that day and night for certain, just as I cried for my verdict and was still crying. It was also due to another verdict dated 1996 whose details resembled the catastrophe of the helicopter. It has lead me to question whether the verdict is destined or that destiny is the verdict. Of course there will always be philosophers who reject the concept of destiny, they do not believe in it at all. Destined matters are called verdicts or as you like it; destiny, hammer, verdict, poisoned arrow, or headache etc. In any case, when it comes, it strikes a blow; it is punctual and sometimes fatal. We have to be careful and take precautions like my verdict. It knocked me down and bled my heart, it ambushed me by surprise...it nearly killed me.

My wound was still opened and exposed to the putrid air. I received many verdicts in my life and they all nearly killed me, they all knocked me out. The one that will kill me has yet to be pronounced. Me, I call destiny, anything around me. Sometimes it brushes by me, other times it knocks me out. How are we to know exactly what is destiny and what is not destiny? This controversial enigma is in fact very simple. What is destiny, we will confirm tomorrow. It is like taking the train tomorrow, we buy the ticket today. But buying the ticket and making a sincere intention to embark on the train is not sufficient enough to secure a seat in that train and to arrive at the desired destination.

Today and still nothing is certain. It is only when we board the train, and the train starts, that we can only confirm the destiny that the train has departed....

Destiny does not condemn us, it does not force us, and it observes us. Ultimately we have the choice, a real choice then afterwards comes the act, and destiny's role is only there to witness the act. We do not make destiny what it is, we only confirm it. Resistance is futile, nobody will beat it. So we all are condemned by this verdict, but not condemned by this verdict in terms of guilt or innocence, being or not being...

The king, queen, prince, president of state, minister, judge, jury member, me, you, everyone trailing behind them, all of us. We all cannot escape the verdict and await it, whether we want it or not, the ultimate verdict which the whole world dreads is, death. Death is the last, big, incriminating verdict, which clutches our life and is also the prize winner of all those small verdicts. Death is also the verdict, which clutches everyone's destiny. Whether he be king, poor, sick, miserable man like me, no one is infallible, it does not discriminate.

I breathe, I yawn, I sigh I am obliged in all these things. But insulting or spitting on someone, we have a huge array of choice. Since I was chained to this world I keep fleeing from death. I fled away from it on many occasions. Death is that magnet, cold and cruel which fascinates me and am attracted towards it against my

will. My body is driftwood, which is under the mercy of that force that current, which tears me and slams me on the rocky reefs sooner or later.

This is such a way that my life ends, by leaving room for others.

THE END

FORTHCOMING BOOKS
BY ELIAS ADAM

THE SICK WORLD
THE POOR OF THE CAMP
EL CHATARRA AND THE FORGOTTEN

(THE BACK COVER)

www.ingramcontent.com/pod-product-compliance
Lightning Source LLC
Chambersburg PA
CBHW021110080526
44587CB00010B/467